Berthoud Library District

ISSUES THAT CONCERN YOU

Date Rape

Norah Piehl, *Book Editor*

Berthoud Community
Library District
236 Welch Ave
(970) 532 2757

GREENHAVEN PRESS

A part of Gale, Cengage Learning

GALE
CENGAGE Learning·

Detroit • New York • San Francisco • New Haven, Conn • Waterville, Maine • London

GALE
CENGAGE Learning·

Elizabeth Des Chenes, *Director, Publishing Solutions*

© 2013 Greenhaven Press, a part of Gale, Cengage Learning

Gale and Greenhaven Press are registered trademarks used herein under license.

For more information, contact:
Greenhaven Press
27500 Drake Rd.
Farmington Hills, MI 48331-3535
Or you can visit our Internet site at gale.cengage.com

For product information and technology assistance, contact us at

Gale Customer Support, 1-800-877-4253
For permission to use material from this text or product, submit all requests online at www.cengage.com/permissions

Further permissions questions can be e-mailed to permissionrequest@cengage.com

Articles in Greenhaven Press anthologies are often edited for length to meet page requirements. In addition, original titles of these works are changed to clearly present the main thesis and to explicitly indicate the author's opinion. Every effort is made to ensure that Greenhaven Press accurately reflects the original intent of the authors. Every effort has been made to trace the owners of copyrighted material.

Cover image © Monkey Business Images/Shutterstock.com

LIBRARY OF CONGRESS CATALOGING-IN-PUBLICATION DATA

Date rape / Norah Piehl, book editor.
    p. cm. -- (Issues that concern you)
 Includes bibliographical references and index.
 ISBN 978-0-7377-6287-7 (hardcover)
 1. Date rape--United States. I. Piehl, Norah.
 HV6561.D373 2012
 364.15'32--dc23
                                                    2012018755

Printed in the United States of America
1 2 3 4 5 6 7 16 15 14 13 12

CONTENTS

According to a national study of college students, rape, including date rape, is perpetrated most commonly against women between the ages of sixteen and twenty-four, and 57 percent of rapes among college women occurred on a date. Clearly date rape education and prevention programs need to start early, to try to prevent violence before it can start. But what is the best approach to address this pervasive and complicated issue?

Several nonprofit organizations conduct programs designed to educate young people—even very young people—about the definition and prevention of date rape. A multiyear program at schools in New South Wales, Australia, for example, takes a holistic approach. School educators begin by focusing on the issues of maintaining respect and forming good relationships, topics that children as young as kindergarten age can understand, years before specific language about sex and rape needs to be introduced. In this program, education specifically about sexual violence and date rape is introduced gradually to older children, alongside such issues as confronting bullying and developing strong, mutually respectful friendships.

Many education programs are structured around confronting myths and misinformation about date rape. One program developed by Advocates for Youth, for example, starts by having high schoolers work in pairs to complete a Quiz on Sexual Violence, which includes true/false statements such as "Sexual violence is most likely to occur to teens in inner city schools," and "While date rape does happen in high schools and colleges, stranger rape happens much more frequently." The workshop facilitator then provides answers and related statistics for each statement (both of the above statements are false) and encourages large-group discussion in response to the facts. Since surveys show that college men often fail to identify their own actions as rape, this approach may help raise awareness and reduce misinformation about what rape looks like.

Students at the University of Southern Indiana, some men wearing high heels, participate in the Walk a Mile in Her Shoes march to stop rape, sexual assault, and gender violence.

Some awareness programs take an unconventional approach to education. Actress and activist Meghan Gardiner, for example, has created a one-woman show called "Dissolve" that aims both to surprise and educate audience members about the issue of drug-assisted date rape. Often, young audiences are not informed about the topic of "Dissolve" before Meghan stages her production at a high school; instead, their surprise about the subject matter evolves alongside their own emotional responses. Similarly, an online interactive video titled "Far from the Heart" allows viewers to virtually attend a party and attempt to keep the video's heroine safe from sexual violence.

Teenage boys and young men can be both perpetrators and victims of date and acquaintance rape. Several organizations, including groups organized and led by men on college campuses, focus their energy and attention on raising awareness among young men and boys. Men Can Stop Rape, for example, has as its mission "to mobilize men to use their strength for creating cultures free from violence, especially men's violence against women." Instead of labeling men as "the problem" with rape and sexual violence, Men Can Stop Rape enlists young men as allies and equal partners, making positive and respectful choices that can result in safer, more equitable relationships for everyone. Men Can Stop Rape offers a variety of multiweek education and prevention programs for students from middle school through college, with the goal of redefining masculinity to focus on healthier, nonviolent models of strength and manhood. According to evaluations funded by the Centers for Disease Control and Prevention, students who complete these prevention programs are significantly less likely to bully and harass their peers and more likely to intervene when they observe both male and female peers being harassed, threatened, or touched inappropriately.

Some communities face particular cultural challenges when it comes to addressing, and educating young people about, date rape. According to the National Organization for Women, for example, Native American women face the highest rate of violence—including sexual violence—of any group in the United States. Addressing this issue is compounded by cultural distrust of law enforcement. On the Yankton Sioux Reservation in South Dakota, for example, a cycle of domestic violence has been working its way into younger and younger generations, resulting in a significant rate of date rape and dating violence. The Native American Women's Health Education Resource Center has formulated a successful program that has brought together adult counselors and educators with members of a teen advisory committee. The teens speak to their peers at domestic violence shelters, community centers, and schools, offering real-life insight into unhealthy relationships and unsafe situations backed up with the authority and professional guidance of their adult mentors. "We want to be able to prevent the trauma before it occurs," notes center director Charon Asetoyer. The issue might be particularly critical in the Native American population, but Asetoyer's sentiments are shared by everyone hoping to increase awareness, and decrease the prevalence, of date rape.

ONE

Date Rape Is Frequently Misunderstood

Sabrina Rubin Erdely

> The process of reporting and prosecuting rapes is made even more complicated when the victim knows her attacker, as Sabrina Rubin Erdely explores in this account. She profiles the victims of an accused serial rapist (known in the media as the Match.com rapist) and the many hurdles involved in charging and convicting him, especially in the state of Pennsylvania, which has extremely restrictive laws about the kinds of evidence and testimony that is and is not admissible in rape trials. Erdely's account illustrates the emotional, legal, and bureaucratic barriers—both official and informal—that often discourage the victims of acquaintance rape from stepping forward and speaking out.
>
> Sabrina Rubin Erdely is an award-winning writer and investigative journalist. Her writing has appeared in the *New Yorker*, *Glamour*, *Men's Health*, *Mother Jones*, and *Self*, among other publications. Her specialty is long-form narrative pieces about crime and health.

Leigh thought her date was going quite well, right up until the point, she says, when she was drugged and raped. It was her first time meeting Jeffrey Marsalis, a gregarious trauma surgeon who had contacted her through the online dating site Match.com. Tall,

Sabrina Rubin Erdely, "The Crime Against Women That No One Understands," *Self*, vol. 30, November 2008. All rights reserved. Reproduced by permission.

blue-eyed and engaging, Marsalis had taken her out in downtown Philadelphia, entertaining her with stories of life in the ER [emergency room]. "He seemed a little full of himself," Leigh recalls; still, she was having a good time. She slowly drank one beer, then a second. Their date was in its fourth hour when Marsalis ordered a carafe of white wine, and Leigh excused herself.

"I would never think to be so cynical that I'd stand there and watch as he poured my drink," remembers Leigh, a striking blonde (who, like all accusers in this article, is identified by her middle name). When the 28-year-old accountant returned to her barstool, her glass of wine was waiting. Leigh took a sip.

Awakening Confused

As she would later testify, the next thing Leigh remembers [was that] she was in a dark room, facedown on a bed—and Marsalis was anally raping her. The pain felt as if he were ripping her in two. Her limbs were leaden, her mind sluggish. "Stop, please stop," Leigh mumbled. Marsalis simply chuckled. Leigh slid back into unconsciousness but kept resurfacing that endless night to discover Marsalis violating her limp body. Finally, she opened her eyes to an apartment filled with late-morning light.

"Good morning," Marsalis said, smiling and leaning in for a kiss; Leigh, stunned, kissed him back. "I had a wonderful time last night. I hope you did, too," she says he told her, staring into her eyes. Leigh felt groggy and confused as she pulled on her jeans. So when Marsalis walked Leigh to her car and suggested they get together again, Leigh heard herself say, "Sure." She was certain she hadn't gone to bed with her date of her own volition—and that she couldn't possibly have blacked out after barely three drinks—but her certainty was softening in the face of his chivalry. *Am I reading the situation wrong?* Leigh wondered as she drove herself home. *Would a rapist act this nicely?*

A Disturbing Truth

Baffling as her experience seemed on that day in February 2005, Leigh was only the latest woman to struggle with the same confu-

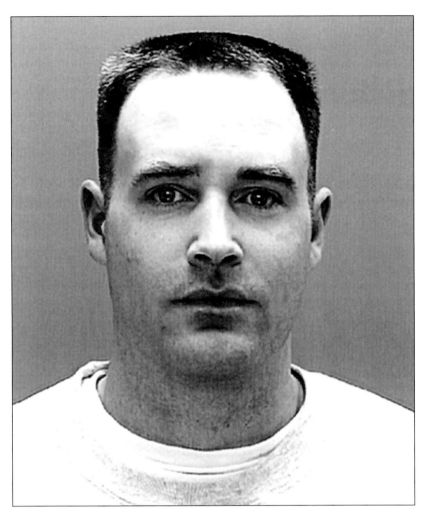

The author was drugged and date raped by Jeffrey Marsalis (pictured). Marsalis was later convicted of date raping several women and is serving a life sentence.

sion. Because Jeffrey Marsalis wasn't really an ER doctor looking for love. He was an unemployed paramedic and nursing-school dropout whose true profession, prosecutors assert, was full-time predator. Investigators would discover 21 women who claimed Marsalis drugged and raped them—many listed in a file on his computer called "The Yearly Calendar of Women." Authorities suspect his true tally is far higher. "Any woman was potential prey," says Philadelphia special prosecutor Joseph Khan. "Plenty of women were attracted to him, but this guy was aroused by the very idea of nonconsent."

As Leigh drove home that morning, she had no idea what lay in her future: that she would join 9 of those 21 accusers to face Marsalis in Philadelphia courtrooms over the course of two trials, telling nearly identical stories of assault. They would be 10 educated, professional women versus a demonstrated liar—a man who had pretended to be a doctor, a CIA employee, even an astronaut—whom a court-appointed psychologist would decide met the legal definition of a "sexually violent predator." And yet the most remarkable thing about both trials wasn't the way they exposed the alleged tactics of a serial date rapist. It was that despite the outrageousness of the accusations against Marsalis, the testimony of 10 women wasn't enough to get a single rape conviction against him. The verdicts in these cases would be far lighter than his accusers sought—and victims' advocates say the outcome reveals a disturbing truth about the justice system. Nationwide, despite all the legal advances of the past three decades, little has changed for women who report a date rape. Because in far too many instances, juries don't believe date rape exists.

Far to Go

When it comes to rape prosecutions as a whole, so much has changed for the better: Thirty years' worth of advocacy, better investigation techniques and tighter laws have led more women than ever to come forward and report the crime to police. But in cases of nonstranger rape—which represent three quarters of all rape cases in the United States—all that progress often comes screeching to a halt in the deliberation room. "Cases where a victim knows her assailant are still extraordinarily hard to win," says Jennifer Long, director of the National Center for the Prosecution of Violence Against Women in Alexandria, Virginia. "Juries are extremely resistant."

Until now, it's been impossible to know exactly how many of these cases collapse in court, because no prosecution data was being collected. But the research and training group End Violence Against Women [EVAW] International in Addy, Washington, just completed a four-year study across eight states and has allowed *SELF* an exclusive early look at its conclusions. Of all the rape cases that come across prosecutors' desks, stranger-rape cases have the best courtroom odds, with 68 percent ending with a conviction or guilty plea. But when a woman knows her assailant briefly (less than 24 hours), a mere 43 percent of cases end in a conviction. When they know each other longer than 24 hours, the conviction rate falls to 35 percent. Even fewer, 29 percent, of intimate partners and exes are punished. "And keep in mind, the cases that come through the prosecutor's door are the strongest ones—strong enough for the police to have referred them along in the first place," notes EVAW International research director Kimberly Lonsway, Ph.D.

Changing Definitions

Back in the 1970s, most reported rapes were committed by strangers; those cases are now in the minority. Yet juries—and many judges as well—still think of rape as being only between strangers, says Lynn Hecht Schafran, director of the National Judicial Education Program of Legal Momentum, a woman's advocacy group in New York City. "To a juror, a rapist is a guy who jumps out of the bushes and throws a woman to the ground," Schafran explains. "She has terrible injuries, and she leaps up and reports it immediately to the police. Anything that falls short of that story is questionable."

Incredibly, that analysis holds true even in a situation as extreme as that of Marsalis. What's especially troubling is that the very things that some of his accusers speculate made the juries so skeptical are typical elements of nonstranger assaults. It doesn't fit with most people's misguided concept of rape, for example, that Marsalis's accusers went out with him willingly—thinking him a worldly doctor, the embodiment of Mr. Right—and were initially enjoying their evening with him. As the defense hammered home, none of the women stormed to the nearest police station or went to a hospital for a rape exam and toxicology test. In fact, the opposite happened: In a near-masochistic twist, most of Marsalis's dates had contact with him again—behavior that seems too bizarre to be believed, but that psychologists say is actually not uncommon among women raped by someone they know. Nonstranger rape is a distinct crime whose survivors exhibit equally distinct behaviors—the very actions the Marsalis defense used against his accusers. It makes you wonder: If these 10 women didn't get a satisfying result, what chance does anyone have in a date rape case?

Finding Courage

"You hate to tell people that we have such terrible success with these cases at trial, because it makes victims think, Well then, why press charges?" says retired police sergeant Joanne Archambault, president and training director of Sexual Assault Training and Investigations, also in Addy, Washington, a firm that educates law enforcement about rape. "But the truth is, until we change the public's attitude about how they see women and sexual violence, we're going to keep losing."

Two days after Leigh awoke in Marsalis's bed, she found herself seated across the table from him at a Chinese restaurant. This is not a date, she reassured herself; rather, it was a fact-finding mission. "I wanted to confront him about what happened. I needed to figure out what was going on," Leigh remembers. She hadn't told anyone she feared she'd been raped. She needed more information first, some validation of her suspicions. "And all that went wrong," Leigh whispers, eyes glazing with tears.

The last thing Leigh says she remembers about that dinner, she was picking at the noodles Marsalis was dishing from a serving plate, trying to muster up her courage to ask: Did you rape me? Then, she says, she blacked out. As Leigh would later tell the court, she woke up in Marsalis's bed again. He was on top of her, once again having sex with her inert body. "It was just devastating," Leigh says. She spends a long moment composing herself, tucking wisps of hair behind her ears. "I made the stupidest decision to go out with him that second time," she says finally. "I think to myself all the time, How could I have done something like that? But I did."

How could Leigh have done such a thing? The idea of reaching out to one's rapist seems like nothing any woman in her right mind would do. Yet the majority of the 10 women who ultimately testified against Marsalis had contact with him afterward. One 33-year-old woman testified that, after regaining consciousness in Marsalis's apartment, she discovered his bed was soaked with her menstrual blood, humiliating her; she later FedExed Marsalis a set of sheets. Two of his accusers befriended him. Two others went on to briefly date Marsalis. Yet another accuser, a 26-year-old pharmaceutical representative, told the court that the assault left her pregnant—and she allowed Marsalis, of all people, to accompany her to the abortion.

Understandable Reactions

"There are so many reasons why victims reengage offenders," says Veronique Valliere, a clinical psychologist in Fogelsville, Pennsylvania, who specializes in sexual abuse. By establishing a relationship on her own terms, a person feeling helpless can reclaim her lost dignity. "Someone yanks that sense of control from you, and you need to get it back," Valliere explains. Denial also plays a powerful role, as many survivors have a hard time accepting the idea of themselves as a victim—and turn to their attackers to help explain away their fears. "We can't believe someone would do something so terrible to us," Valliere says. "We work under the assumption that this must be something we can understand through talking it over." It's the classic female response to tackling a problem: Let's discuss it.

Marsalis's accusers may have been especially prone to have further contact with him because in many cases their memories of those nights were foggy. And prosecutors argue that Marsalis skillfully exploited that confusion. In interviews with *SELF*, one accuser described how it unfolded: In October 2003, Marie was a 23-year-old grad student living in Marsalis's building when one evening, she ran into her neighbor "Dr. Jeff." Marsalis asked her out for a drink at a nearby bar. Two gin and tonics later, she would testify, it was suddenly sunrise, and Marie was naked from the waist down in Marsalis's bed. "I was bleeding and hurting," she remembers. "But I just didn't remember anything. And I didn't want to acknowledge that I'd been raped." The whole thing didn't make sense to her—she'd never blacked out before in her life—so Marie got out of there as fast as she politely could and avoided Marsalis for several weeks. But when she came face-to-face with him at the building's Christmas party, she acted perfectly friendly. "Talking to him, I guess it was a way of asserting myself, an attempt to restore some normalcy," Marie says. "I was trying to be logical instead of emotional."

Nevertheless, Marie's subconscious couldn't forget. She began withdrawing socially and starving herself. A 5-foot, 100-pound pixie to begin with, Marie lost so much weight that within three months, she was hospitalized for a heart arrhythmia. As she lay in the ER, it occurred to Marie that Marsalis had said he worked at that very same hospital.

"I called him," she says hollowly. And Marsalis visited her, playing the role of doctor by wearing a stethoscope and flipping through her chart. Two days later, after Marie had gone home, the "doctor" showed up at her apartment to check on her. Then, as Marie would tell the court, Marsalis steered her to her bed, pinned her down and raped her again. This time, there was no blackout to cloud her perception; Marsalis offered no smooth talk as he pulled up his scrubs and left. Marie made her way to the shower, curled up under the water and cried. Yet she didn't even consider calling the police.

Reasons Not to Report

Think most women would behave differently—that in the same situation, they would jump up and call 911? Think again. According to government estimates, a mere 19 percent of rapes, including stranger rapes, are ever reported in the first place. As Valliere notes, women who have been sexually assaulted find so

Rape Victims and the Justice System

Reporting Rape to the Police
Percent of rapes reported

Rapist was intimate

82%
Not repor...

18%
...ed

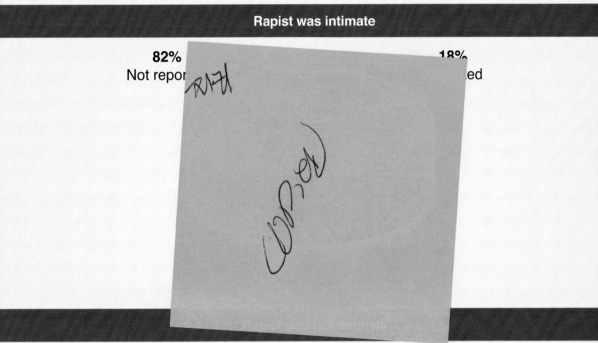

79.1%
Not reported

20.9%
Reported

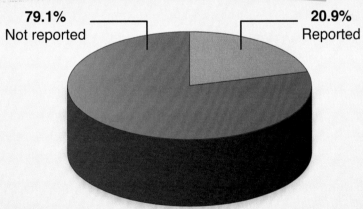

many reasons not to call police, including denial, shame or their hazy grasp of the facts due to drugs or alcohol. Many survivors assume they won't be believed. Still others, such as Marie and Leigh, are mortified into silence by what they see as their complicity in their own attacks. "I brought myself to this situation," Leigh explains, voice surging with emotion. "And I had done it not once, but twice. Who in the world's gonna believe that?"

Leigh never called the police. Instead, she did her best to move on. She forced herself to date again on Match.com—"I didn't want to be afraid," she says—where she soon met a man and fell in love. In September 2006, Leigh had been engaged for three days when she got a call from an FBI agent. "He said in a voice mail that it's about a man I dated from Match," she recalls. "And I knew, immediately." Leigh met with the agent in his Philadelphia office and poured out the story she'd been holding back for so long. It was only then that Leigh learned who Jeffrey Marsalis really was and why investigators were so keen on speaking with her.

The agent told Leigh that Marsalis had recently been tried for the rapes of three other women. The first accuser had called the police in March 2005—roughly two weeks after Leigh's attack. She was a 25-year-old pharmacist, a religious woman who had been saving her virginity for marriage until, she would testify, she had blacked out during a date with Marsalis and had awoken underneath him. In a surprising turn of events, when police showed up at Marsalis's apartment with a search warrant, the building's 29-year-old manager had blanched—and blurted, unprompted, that Marsalis had drugged and raped her, too. Up in Marsalis's apartment, law enforcement collected his computer; they realized they had an even bigger case when they found "The Yearly Calendar of Women," listing some 58 first names, and other files with contact information. Among them was a 27-year-old lawyer who told an uncannily similar tale.

A Tough Case

The following January, all three of the women had taken the stand in *Commonwealth of Pennsylvania v. Jeffrey Marsalis*. By uniting them in a single trial, the Philadelphia district attorney's office had hoped to prove a pattern of predation, to erase any doubts a jury might have. But during the weeklong trial, the case had come undone. For one thing, the defense denied that Marsalis drugged the women, and there was no physical evidence to support that accusation. Police had found a syringe of liquid diphenhydramine in Marsalis's apartment, a drug that can cause powerful sleepiness, and theorized that he'd used expired medications he'd had access to at school or work. But testing was not completed and the syringe was not introduced as evidence. Plus, none of the accusers had gotten a toxicology screening—which presumably wouldn't have turned up anything anyway, because the drug would have left their system quickly. It was the behavior of the women, however, that the defense used to truly torpedo the case. The apartment manager had become friends with Marsalis. The attorney had gone on to have a short relationship with him. Neither had immediately called police or gone to a hospital for a rape-kit exam. As for the pharmacist, she had waited more than a month to make a report.

The jury had acquitted Marsalis on all counts. Even so, moments after the jury read the not-guilty verdict, Marsalis was rearrested right in the courtroom: He had new charges to face. Already in custody during his first trial, he was denied bail again and sent immediately back to jail.

"Something I Had to Do"

Prosecutor Joseph Khan urged Leigh to join this second trial, for which they planned to combine the strongest cases among Marsalis's long list of accusers. Marie, too, was contacted by the D.A.'s office. She was reluctant, but they told her that her story was compelling enough to bolster the other cases. "I wouldn't have done it if it was just me," Marie says. "But because I could help the others, I felt it was something I had to do." So the two women joined five others to face down Marsalis in court. They had safety in numbers; no way could they lose this time.

"Jeffrey is a playboy," said defense attorney Kevin Hexstall, speaking to the jury in June 2007. "You don't have to like him for that, but you got to respect and understand the fact that's all he is."

The core of the defense's theory was simple: All seven women were lying. Each had gotten drunk, had consensual sex with Marsalis and regretted it. Then, when authorities called them and revealed that Marsalis had lied about his profession, they felt betrayed and cried rape as revenge. "This is not the forum for that!" Hexstall told the jury in his closing argument. "Throw a brick through his car window, slash his tires. Get online and tell the rest of the world he's not a doctor. . . . You don't come up with this kind of nonsense and play with this man's life!"

The jury sat rapt. "Let's think about what some of the real patterns are, and some of the real similarities in these cases," Hexstall boomed. "All of these women wanted to date Jeffrey Marsalis," he said. "They all went out drinking. Nobody said, 'Let's catch a movie, we want to go to a ball game, let's just have dinner, let's meet in the park, I just want to talk.' They all went out with Dr. Jeff, and they all went out drinking alcohol."

Perpetuating Myths

Although rape-shield laws protect women from having their sexual past discussed at trial, acquaintance-rape defenses continue to "play into these myths about how 'good' women act versus 'bad' girls," Long says. "And that it's the risky behavior of the 'bad' girls that somehow invites a rape." Trials often hinge not on the behavior of the defendant, but rather on whether the woman did enough to protect herself from his advances. From that point of view, Marsalis's seven accusers had done everything wrong. "We were definitely on trial," Marie comments drily. "If it was the 1600s, it would have been a stoning."

The women's composure may not have helped their standing with the jury. Although a couple of them became emotional during their testimony—including Marie, who blotted her eyes and took breathers—most, like Leigh, kept it together. But experts say many jurors expect women to weep when they are talking about a rape. "If you don't cry, it means nothing happened to you," says

Legal Momentum's Schafran. "Of course, if you cry too much, you're too hysterical to be believed." (Hexstall reminded the jury that one woman had cried while testifying about her abortion, but not while discussing the alleged rape—proof, he claimed, that the sex had been consensual.) The fact that many of the women had continued to function in their everyday life was further evidence that nothing had occurred. "Rape is the only crime where victims aren't allowed to be OK," says psychologist Valliere, who points out that in cases of car theft, for example, the theft's emotional impact doesn't factor into the verdict—only whether the car was taken against the victim's will. "But if someone is raped and seems OK, we say, 'Could that really have been a rape?'"

Limiting Testimony

It's a given, too, that no one on a rape jury has any real insight into the crime or its consequences, because during the jury-selection process lawyers routinely weed out almost anyone who admits to real-life experience with sexual assault. Clouding matters further, Pennsylvania law forbids the use of expert testimony to explain the behavior of rape victims (a policy state legislators are trying to change, as a result of outcry over this case). So the Marsalis jury had little context in which to understand the lurid, difficult-to-digest details they were hearing.

Judge Steven Geroff also wouldn't allow witness testimony from yet another accuser, a woman who had worked with Marsalis at an Idaho ski resort. And in one final confusing stroke, right before jurors headed into the deliberation room, they were read a jury instruction—antiquated and misleading yet still standard in Pennsylvania—saying in part that the women's failure to immediately report their assault "should be considered" in the jury's decision.

A Shocking Decision

When the jury returned after five days, it proclaimed Marsalis not guilty of eight of the nine counts of rape he was facing. They had deadlocked on the remaining charge, unable to decide whether Marie's second, violent encounter had indeed been a rape. Instead, the jury opted to find Marsalis guilty of two counts of the lesser charge of sexual assault. One assault conviction was for Marie's second attack. The other conviction was for the case of a 26-year-old advertising exec who, upon waking in Marsalis's bed in the middle of the night, had driven herself home; when Marsalis had called to apologize for "things getting out of hand," she had refused to see him again. She was the only one of the seven women who had called police—albeit four years later, after she saw a TV news report of Marsalis's courtroom rearrest.

The jury isn't talking, but courtroom observers have a theory about why the jury chose to believe these two women above the other five: Their behaviors fit best with the rape-victim stereotype. Both had welled up while testifying and described lasting emotional damage. They were also the slightest physically of the accusers; in a parade of strikingly put-together women, they may have come across as most vulnerable. And so the jury seemed willing to acknowledge that something had happened to them—although whatever it was, it didn't rise to the level of rape. As for the other five accusers, including Leigh, the jury concluded that no crime at all had been committed against them.

"Twelve people looked me in the face and called me a liar," Leigh says softly, hugging her knees at the kitchen table of the apartment she shares with her husband. "I put myself out there. I told them every terrible detail. And they said no." Even Marie, who had the most positive verdict, felt cheated, especially when she realized she'd have to endure a retrial on the hung rape charge. As she watched footage of jurors sprinting from the courtroom, some shielding their face, Marie became enraged. "If you're going to make a decision that affects people's lives, tell us why you decided what you did," she demands. "Don't go running out of there, hiding your face like you're ashamed!"

In the end, Marsalis took a plea deal to avoid a retrial: Prosecutors agreed to drop Marie's remaining rape charge in exchange for Marsalis pleading no contest to a charge of "unlawful restraint" for yet another accuser who had not been part of either trial. "They used my hung charge to get some vindication for her, which she wouldn't have gotten otherwise. So that made it worth it," Marie says.

"A Wolf in Sheep's Clothing"

Although Marsalis faced as little as community service, at his sentencing hearing, Judge Geroff delivered a stronger message than the jury had: He sentenced Marsalis to 10.5 to 21 years behind bars plus 4 years probation, the maximum allowed, and noted that he'll face mandatory Megan's Law registration for the rest of his life. "What you were was a wolf in sheep's clothing," Geroff told Marsalis from the bench. "Your lifestyle was a fantasy. What's happened to your victims is reality." Seated together in two rows at the front of the courtroom, a group of Marsalis's accusers smiled with relief, some through tears. The sentencing softened the blow of the disappointing verdict; finally, their combined efforts had yielded something. "At least he's locked away, and I know he won't do this to anyone else. Without all of us there, that might not have happened," Leigh says. "And of course, all this isn't even over yet," she adds.

Because in January, Marsalis heads to a courtroom to be tried for rape a third time. Court documents filed by the D.A. in the Philadelphia cases describe the accuser's story: Back in late September 2005, shortly before his first trial was to begin, Marsalis made his way to Idaho, where he took a job as a security guard at a ski resort. There he invited a 21-year-old coworker to join him for a drink at a local bar. Over beers, she told him she wasn't interested in him romantically—she was a lesbian. Marsalis ordered another round and handed her a kamikaze. She noticed a sugary-looking residue at the bottom of the glass; when she drank it down, however, it tasted bitter, not sweet. The rest of her story unfolds in a now-familiar way: She awoke the next day in Marsalis's bed, feeling sore and nauseated. He graciously walked her back to her dorm, chatting the whole way and leaving her with the suggestion that they "hang out sometime."

New Hope

Instead, this accuser did something unusual: She contacted the police. Then she had a rape kit done. The prompt investigation turned up eyewitnesses who said they had seen Marsalis dragging her, barely coherent, out of a taxi while she mumbled, "No, I'm going to stay here." And when police confronted Marsalis, he initially denied having sex with her. "She is more of a manly type of a woman for one," he told police. "If I was going to have sex with somebody, wouldn't I have picked someone who is some drop-dead gorgeous woman? You think?"

This case has it all, it seems, everything to erase doubt from the mind of a juror: prompt reporting, physical evidence, eyewitnesses, Marsalis's inconsistent statements to police and, because of the accuser's sexual orientation, no dating behavior to confuse a jury. In other words, her case bears no resemblance at all to a typical report of nonstranger rape. And that is exactly why experts predict that this time around, the woman taking the stand will finally win. [Editor's note: Marsalis was convicted in July 2009 and because of his previous history, sentenced to life in prison.]

TWO

Date Rape Carries Long-Lasting Consequences for Individuals

Nirvana Gonzalez Rosa

Although acquaintance rape is frustratingly common, its effects, which can be long lasting, will vary by individual and can often last for years, even for a lifetime. This piece outlines acute and chronic emotional, mental, and physical consequences of rape in general, and date rape in particular. These consequences can range from anxiety and depression to alcohol abuse and sleep disorders. The author also debunks common myths surrounding acquaintance rape and includes guidance for mental health providers working with these victims.

Nirvana Gonzalez Rosa is the general coordinator of the Latin American and Caribbean Women's Health Network, a nongovernmental organization that brings together organizations and individuals involved in the women's health movement and other social movements to promote universal access to comprehensive health care. She has worked as a consultant on issues of domestic and sexual violence and as a community organizer addressing issues such as sexuality and HIV/AIDS in her native Puerto Rico and throughout Latin America and the Caribbean.

Nirvana Gonzalez Rosa, "A Rape by Any Other Name . . . The Truth and Consequences of 'Date Rape,'" *Women's Health Journal,* vol. 2010, January–June, 2010. Copyright © 2010 Rodale, Inc. All rights reserved. Reproduced by permission.

"Date rape" is sexual violence perpetrated by a "friend" in the context of a social outing. He could be a schoolmate, a colleague from work, a boyfriend or an acquaintance. He is someone the woman knows and with whom she is willing to spend time with, but the "date" culminates with sexual assault or rape. Studies carried out in the United States show that:

- 12% of all rapes occur in the context of a date. (Russell, 1984).
- 75–85% of all sexual aggressors are known to their victims.
- In 2001, the Illinois Coalition Against Sexual Assault surveyed 6,000 students at 32 universities and found that one of every six women is raped during the school year; 84% of the survivors knew their attacker; 57% of the rapes occurred on a date; only 27% of the women considered themselves victims of rape, even though the sexual violence met the legal definition of rape; and 42% of the women who had been raped had not told anyone about the assault.
- 20–25% of all female university students will be the victims of sexual assault at some time during their studies.
- One out of five female students state that they had been forced to have sexual relations.
- 91% of the survivors who report sexual assaults are women.
- Three out of every 100 female university students will be raped or will experience an attempted rape during the school year. (Department of Justice, Washington, D.C., 2000).

Date rape is most often reported by young women who are college students, but any woman can be a victim of this type of sexual assault.

Impact on Comprehensive Health

The psychological and emotional impact of rape varies with each individual. Women who have been raped by their boyfriend or acquaintance in the context of a date suffer many of the same fears and other feelings endured by victims of any other type of sexual assault, such as guilt or insecurity. They may feel betrayed or believe that somehow they "provoked" the rape. As a result, rape survivors face a series of psychological consequences that require careful treatment, so that they can recover their ability to trust in others as well as in themselves. In fact, feelings of guilt may be even more common and intense in the case of date rape than when the sexual assault is perpetrated by a stranger. This guilt is one of the most difficult consequences to overcome, especially if the survivor does not get professional help.

Regardless of the circumstances in which it occurs, sexual violence leaves profound scars on women's lives. If a woman agrees to go out for a drink, a walk on the beach or a stroll through the park, during the day or at night, but then doesn't want to have sex, her decision will often be met with protest, a denial followed by arguments to convince her that she really wants it. This is the socially scripted game of seduction: when a woman says no to sex, she really means yes. And since sex on the first date and sexual aggression in women are not condoned by society, the man often thinks that he should insist, coerce and even use force, if necessary.

In general, survivors of sexual violence present chronic health problems that include:

- Rape trauma syndrome, which is manifest in somatic, cognitive, psychological and behavioral symptoms and is usually expressed in two stages: the acute stage and the outward adjustment stage.
- Post-traumatic stress disorder;
- Social phobias (especially in the case of survivors of date or marital rape);
- Frequent drug use or drug abuse;
- Suicidal behavior.

The medium- to long-range consequences of rape include:

- Chronic headaches;
- Fatigue;
- Sleep disturbances (nightmares or recurring dreams of the crime);
- Nausea;
- Eating disorders;
- Pain during menstruation;
- Sexual dysfunction.

The acute stage of rape trauma syndrome is a crisis period that occurs immediately after the attack and lasts for about two or three weeks. In this stage, the rape survivor usually feels strong emotions and physical symptoms. The emotional responses can be expressed openly or may be contained. These responses can range from nervousness, tearfulness and sobbing to smiling and laughing to presenting a calm, controlled demeanor.

Some of the most commonly expressed emotions are anger, fear, anxiety and shock. Rape victims also often experience rapid changes in mood and feelings of:

- Humiliation;
- Degradation;
- Shame;
- Guilt;
- Defenselessness;
- Rage;
- Hopelessness;
- Desire for revenge;
- Fear of being attacked again.

The outward adjustment stage starts two or three weeks after the rape and begins when the survivor starts the process of reorganizing her life and dealing with the long-term trauma of rape. This process can either be adaptive or maladaptive.

The reactions in this stage vary considerably according to the individual and are also influenced by the circumstances in which the rape occurred, who the rapist was and what sort of treatment the survivor received after the rape. Some survivors of rape make radical changes in their lives, they may quit their job, move or even leave the country. Other survivors develop a phobia of being alone or being in places or situations in which the rape took place. Sexual dysfunction or changes in the survivor's sex life are also very common concerns.

Rape survivors also often experience symptoms of post-traumatic stress disorder, especially those who were threatened with weapons or extreme physical force. The impact of such situations is very powerful, and this trauma may be evidenced in the form of invasive thoughts, such as nightmares or recurring ideas. It may also be manifest in evasive thoughts, like:

- Listlessness;
- Withdrawing from family, friends and associates;
- Being distracted;
- Intellectualizing the experience;
- Increased use of alcohol;
- High-risk behavior;
- Avoiding places, activities or people that remind them of the rape;
- Disassociation;
- Hyperawareness;
- Irritability;
- Panic attacks.

Drugs Used in Date Rape

Drugs are sometimes used to assist in committing a sexual assault. Because of the effects of these "date-rape drugs," victims may be physically helpless, unable to refuse sex and unable to remember what happened. The drugs are easily added to flavored drinks without the victim's knowledge, because they have little or no taste, odor or color. They can leave the victim unable to move or talk, and she may wake up hours later with little or no memory of what happened. When combined with alcohol, these drugs can be lethal. The most common date-rape drugs are GHB, Ketamine and Rohypnol.

GHB is the abbreviation for gamma hydroxybutyric acid. It is a salty liquid with no odor or color, a white powder or a pill. In as little as fifteen minutes, GHB can cause feelings of intoxication and dizziness followed immediately by drowsiness and then profound sedation that can last up to eight hours. GHB slows heart rate and can cause nausea, loss of consciousness, inability to remember what happened while drugged, seizures, coma and even death. Some of the street names for GHB are Grievous Bodily Harm, Liquid G, Liquid Ecstasy, Somatomax, Cherry Meth, Easy Lay and Gamma 10.

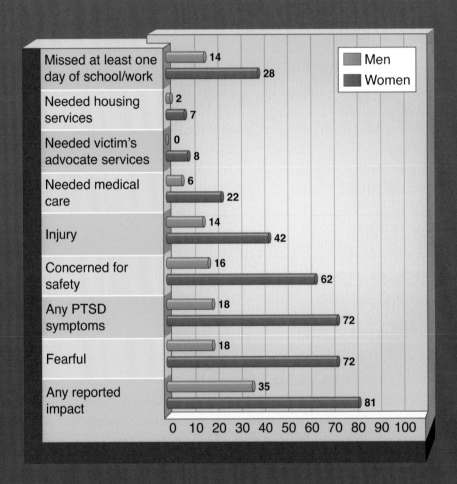

	Men	Women
Missed at least one day of school/work	14	28
Needed housing services	2	7
Needed victim's advocate services	0	8
Needed medical care	6	22
Injury	14	42
Concerned for safety	16	62
Any PTSD symptoms	18	72
Fearful	18	72
Any reported impact	35	81

Taken from: Centers for Disease Control and Prevention National Intimate Partner and Sexual Violence Survey, 2010.

Ketamine (brand name Ketaset or Vetalar): Ketamine is a general anesthetic often used by veterinarians that comes in the form of a liquid, a white powder or a pill. Like GHB, this drug is often used in clubs and at raves because of its euphoric effects. Ketamine can cause hallucinations, lost sense of time and identity, agitation, paranoia, aggressive or violent behavior, convulsions, loss of consciousness, loss of coordination and potentially fatal respiratory failure. In large amounts, it can cause oxygen deprivation in the brain and muscles. The effects of Ketamine usually last for just an hour or so, but they may last as long as four to six hours. Full recuperation takes two full days. Ketamine is also known as Special K, Ket and K, Vitamin K, Kit Kat, Keller, Cat Valium, Purple and Super C.

Rohypnol: Rohypnol is a pill that quickly dissolves in liquid. It is a very potent sedative and, when combined with alcohol, can cause total loss of consciousness. The immediate effects are felt after just ten minutes and also include lower blood pressure, sleepiness, dizziness, muscle relaxation or loss of muscle control, visual disturbances, problems talking, nausea and the inability to remember what happened while drugged. Street names for Rohypnol include Roofies, R2, Roofenol, Roche, Roachies, La Rocha, Rope, Rib, Circles, Mexican Valium, Roach-2, Roopies, Ropies, Forget Pill, Trip-and-Fall and Mind Erasers.

Myth vs. Reality

As in many situations related to violence against women, there are a series of concepts about sexual violence that are not always justified. These notions are often used to defend the aggressor. We must therefore acknowledge the differences between myth and reality.

Myth: If a woman lets a man buy her dinner, a few drinks, takes her to the movies or out dancing, then she should be willing to repay him with sex.

Reality: Sexual relations are not payment for the expenses of a dinner or any other activity, regardless of how much money was spent. It must always be consensual.

Myth: Kissing or fondling means that a penetrative sexual relationship is inevitable.

Reality: Everyone has the right to say "no," and this decision must be respected, regardless of what they had agreed to or had done on some prior occasion.

Myth: Once a man is aroused, he has to have sex and cannot help pressuring or forcing the woman.

Reality: Everyone can control their sexual needs.

Myth: When a woman says "No," at heart, she wants to say "Yes."

Reality: This notion is based on old sexual stereotypes that are still believed, according to which women hide their desire for sex so that they won't appear to be "easy."

Myth: Date rapists are easy to spot.

Reality: Women are usually sexually assaulted by "normal" men on "regular" dates (after having dinner, seeing a movie or going out dancing). In other words, date rapists are apparently trustworthy men.

Myth: If a woman likes to wear "sexy" or sensual attire or she drinks alcohol, then she is risking sexual assault; in other words, it is her fault for "provoking" the man.

Reality: Having a drink or dressing up is not an invitation to commit sexual violence.

Myth: It's better to be raped by someone you know than by a stranger.

Reality: Any sexual violence, can be emotionally traumatic and devastating for the victim, no matter who perpetrates it, and the impact can last for a very long time.

Treatment for Survivors of Sexual Assault

No matter when the sexual assault happened, the survivor needs treatment and support. If she decides to seek help, whether it be psychological counseling or legal advice, the case must be treated as an emergency, with sensitive, confidential, humane and respectful care and by believing the survivor's story.

It is important to make it clear that the rapist was responsible for what happened and that the victim did nothing to provoke the attack. She must also be helped to understand she was not an accomplice to the crime but a victim and that her reactions during the assault were essential for surviving the attack, whether she chose to give in, or to scream, or whatever she did. While some women defend themselves tooth and nail, others adopt a more passive attitude, but no one can say that one response is better than another.

Reporting the crime is a delicate process. Many women prefer not to press charges, because they are scared, feel guilty, don't trust the justice system or are afraid of being mistreated. But the truth is, if they report the rape, there is a better chance that the rapist will not get away with it.

In any case, it is important that the rape survivor be treated by professionals who have experience working with victims of sexual violence so that the healing process can start as soon as possible and so that she can access the services to which she has a right, such as anti-retrovirals to prevent HIV infection, emergency contraception, etc.

In general, during professional interviews with victims of sexual assault, the following precautions should be kept in mind:

- The interview must be carried out in private and without interruption, to the greatest extent possible.
- The survivor must have total freedom to express what happened, either verbally or by crying, if that is what she needs.
- The interviewer should use soft, gentle tones and clear, simple language throughout the interview.
- Lapses of silence and the emotional rhythm of the victim should be respected.
- She must be counseled about her rights and about the legal procedure if she wants to file charges against the person who attacked her.
- The survivor's decision to not share details about the rape, to not file a report or to not press charges must be respected.
- Any expression that implies a value judgment or that blames the survivor must be avoided.

Conclusions

The act of sexual violence known as "date rape" is just that, the crime of rape. Therefore, this term should really not be used because it tends to minimize the seriousness of the crime. In fact, it is never appropriate to define a crime based on the context in which it occurs; for example, when we speak of a mugging, it is never called, "theft of a person who was walking in the street."

"Date rape" is sexual violence. The rapist uses force, drugs, alcohol, threats and/or emotional coercion in the context of a relationship that has just begun or that has been going on for some time.

Most sexual assaults of adults or minors are planned. In fact, rape is the most common premeditated crime following robbery. Rape is not the result of overwhelming passion or sexual desire. Planning a rape is a complex routine, and the rapist will often use very subtle manipulation and intimidation.

Rape is about power, and rapists who attack women that they are dating use a series of justifications to rationalize their behavior: "it was a date . . . she knew what was going to happen" (as if rape were a normal part of dating); "she shouldn't have drunk so much if she didn't want to have sex" (as if trusting someone were an invitation to rape); or "she didn't fight me or scream" (being paralyzed by fear or shock does not constitute consent).

Many women and children are warned every day by their family and authority figures to be careful, to be aware of risks and to not talk with strangers. However, most sexual assaults are perpetrated by people who are known to the victims; no one ever warns you to be careful with your friends, family or acquaintances. It is precisely this factor of familiarity that produces a feeling of safety and trust that makes women, young people and children more vulnerable to a potential rapist.

That is why women often "lower their guard" and fall victim to this sort of crime. In fact, they even doubt that what happened was really rape, because the aggressor was a partner, boyfriend or husband. We have been taught that rape is an act perpetrated by a stranger by means of force, threats or coercion, at a place and time where the woman "shouldn't be." The notion that the woman somehow provoked the rape or that they "deserve" to be raped because they were somewhere they should not have been or they were dressed "inappropriately." But this is just an old prejudice that shifts the blame away from the attacker and does not apply to reality.

Sexual violence that occurs in the context of a date is often the result of socially prescribed sex roles and misunderstood sexual

Date rape is defined as sexual violence perpetrated by a friend or acquaintance in the context of a social outing. It could be a schoolmate, boyfriend, or casual acquaintance.

signals. Some men see sex as a sign of competence and believe that "no" might become "yes" with a little persuasion, psychological pressure, or by force "if necessary." They believe that some girls say "no" because they don't want the man to think badly of them or because they are afraid of becoming pregnant or getting some sexually transmitted infection. However, the reality is that sexual violence begins the moment that someone says no, and this decision is not respected.

Our society is saturated with explicit and subliminal messages about women who "want to be dominated" by a man or who "provoke" a sexual attack, which perpetuates attitudes and behavior that give rise to a struggle for power, control and domination between women and men. Think of all the famous, classic films, as well as the many contemporary soap operas or even literary works in which we see that hackneyed scene of the woman who says "no" to a sexual advance, the "hero" insists and insists, as she continues to refuse him, until finally, in some magical revelation, she melts into his irresistible embrace. She eventually falls in love with her "Prince Charming"—or her rapist? —after he manages to "conquer" her. This sort of message is deeply engrained in the minds of boys and girls from a very early age.

Any form of sex by means of force, coercion, intimidation or threat is a crime, an act of violence and power that violates the victim's body and mutilates her spirit, whether the aggressor is a partner, a friend or a colleague from school or work.

All professionals, especially those who work in sexual health, mental health and the justice system, must be responsible for understanding the truth and consequences of rape. As health-care and legal professionals, they must comprehend rape survivors' realities in order to meet their needs in an appropriate and respectful fashion.

What NOT to Say or Do with a Rape Survivor

- Blame the survivor for the abuse.
- Deny that the abuse occurred and refuse to believe her.
- Express alarm or fear.
- Assume an overprotective attitude.
- Ask the survivor to not talk about the rape.
- Make it into a joke and share it with people who are not going to help the survivor.
- Take pity on the survivor and change your behavior towards her.
- Pressure the survivor to report the incident to the police.
- Think that the rape may not have happened because the medical examination didn't find any physical trauma.
- Minimize the abuse because either the survivor or the rapist were under the effects of alcohol, drugs or some mental disorder or disability.

What You Should Do

- Help the survivor understand that she is not to blame and that only the person who attacked her is responsible.
- Try to stay calm.
- Tell her that she was right to talk about it and very brave to do so.
- Let her know that she is not alone, that other people have lived through this experience, too.
- Explain what sort of support or service you can provide, when and up to what point. It is important that she knows your limits.
- Ask the survivor for permission to tell others about the rape, so that they can help.
- Try to offer contained support by creating a network of support made up of a tightly knit group (. . .) and always keep the survivor informed by staying in contact with her.

Source: Servicios Legales de Puerto Rico (SLPR), Guia para el Manejo y Atencion de Sobrevivientes de Agresiones Sexuales.

Possible Behavioral Manifestations of Someone Who Was Sexually Abused as a Child or an Adolescent

- Promiscuity;
- Prostitution;
- Avoidance of sexual arousal;
- Compulsive sexual behavior;
- Memories of the abuse;
- Isolation;
- Drug or alcohol abuse;
- Self-mutilation;
- Suicide attempts;
- Involvement in criminal behavior;
- Aggressive behavior;
- Involvement in abusive relationships;
- Phobias;
- Nightmares;

- Vulnerability to other forms of victimization;
- "Leaving" their body to not feel something;
- Allowing the same thing to happened to their own children;
- Personality disorders;
- Possibility of becoming a sexual aggressor themselves;
- Eating disorders.

Not all people who have experienced sexual abuse will display all of these possible consequences. How they react will depend on a range of factors: their relationship with the aggressor; how many people were involved in the abuse; the age at which it occurred; how many times it occurred; the elements used during the abuse (trickery, coercion, threats, intimidation, manipulation, bribery with gifts or money or use of surprise, force or weapons); the type of sexual abuse; and whether or not they were believed and given support and protection when they shared what had happened.

Undoubtedly, the misinformation and distorted perspective on sexuality that we receive from various sources promotes many sexual problems, among individuals as well as within society.

Source: Servicios Legales de Puerto Rico (SLPR), Guia para el Manejo y Atencion de Sobrevivientes de Agresiones Sexuales.

Other Resources

New York Online Access to Health, www.noah-health.org

SafeTeens—Date Rape Drugs, http:// www.safeteens.org/rape drugs_ text.html

Sexual Violence Research Initiative, www.svri.org

Galimberti, Diana M., "Componentes claves para el diseno de protocolos de atencion a la violencia sexual" (Washington, D.C.: PAHO, 2005), online at http://www.ops-oms.org/ Spanish/AD /GE/SexualViolence Aug05-GalimbertiComponentes.ppt

National Sexual Violence Resource Center, Global Perspectives on Sexual Violence: Findings from the World Report on Violence

and Health (Enola, PA: NSVRC, 2004), online at http://www
.nsvrc.org/publications/ nsvrc-publications/global-perspectives
- sexual-violence-findings-worldreport- violence-a

References

ACTION OHIO Coalition for Battered Women, "Teen Dating
Violence Facts," http://www.abanet.org/unmet/teendating/ facts
.pdf

Centro de Ayuda a Victimas de Violacion, "La violacion en
cita es un crimen." Puerto Rico: Centro de Ayuda a Victimas de
Violacion, Depto de Salud.

Cheryl, Kay and Butler L., Traci, Treatment Strategies for Abused
Children, Activity Book for Treatment Strategies for Abused
Children: From Victim to Survivor. Thousand Oaks, CA: Sage
Publications, 1996.

Gonzalez Rosa, Nirvana, Impacto del Incesto en la Vida de las
Mujeres, en Los Espejos de la Desigualdad, Mujeres y Salud
Mental, Cuadernos Mujer Salud 6 (Santiago, Chile: Red de Salud
de las Mujeres Latinoamericanas y del Caribe) 2001.

Illinois Department of Public Health, "Facts About Date-Rape
Drugs," http:// www.idph.state.il.us/about/ womenshealth/fact
sheets/date.htm

NCVC, "El abuso en citas/aventuras/ relaciones amorosas," http://
www.ncvc. org/tvp/main.aspx?dbID=DB_Abuso_ en_Relaciones
_Amorosas107

Ministerio de Salud Publica, Guatemala, "Protocolo de Atencion
a Victimas de Violencia Sexual." Guatemala: Ministerio de Salud
Publica, 2005.

Portal del Recinto de Ciencias Medicas, UPR, "Que son las dro-
gas para la violacion en citas? www.rcm.upr.edu/rcm/ PrevCMS
/Drogas%20en%20Cita.pdf

Semillas para el Cambio. Boletin Centro de Ayuda a Victimas de
Violacion (Puerto Rico) 3, Mayo 1987.

Servicios Legales de Puerto Rico (SLPR), Guia para el Manejo y Atencion de Sobrevivientes de Agresiones Sexuales.

Soriano, Andres, Hablamos de Maltrato Infantil. Madrid: Editorial San Pablo, 2001.

Rosa, Nirvana Gonzalez

Source Citation

Rosa, Nirvana Gonzalez. "A rape by any other name . . . the truth and consequences of 'date rape'." Women's Health Journal Jan.–June 2010: 40+. General OneFile. Web. 10 Nov. 2011.

Document URL

http://0-go.galegroup.com.luna.wellesley.edu/ps/i.do?&id=GALE%7CA232889045&v=2.1&u=mlin_m_wellcol&it=r&p=ITOF&sw=w

THREE

Rape Accusations Can Impact Schools and Towns

Jessica Bennett

When date rape happens in a small town or involves local celebrities, the effects can go far beyond just a victim and an attacker. Here Jessica Bennett tells the story of Hillaire Soignet, a popular cheerleader who was reportedly raped by an even more popular football star at a party. As Bennett reports, the issues surrounding the case were made more complicated by the fact that the alleged perpetrator was black and his victim was white; in a small town known for its conservatism and racist history, this case achieved notoriety. Another factor was the Texas town's near-reverence for football and the victim's reluctance to cheer for her attacker at subsequent football games. Often this most personal crime has implications that affect victims' and attackers' friends, families, and communities as well.

Jessica Bennett is a senior writer and editor for The Daily Beast web site and *Newsweek* magazine. She frequently writes about social issues, gender, sex, and culture. She has won awards from the New York Press Club, the Gay and Lesbian Alliance Against Defamation, and the Society of Professional Journalists.

She was blonde and blue-eyed, captain of her high-school cheer squad, headstrong, but shy at times, too: she made a point not to call undue attention to herself. He was tall and strapping, an outgoing African-American kid, a church-going boy with the swagger of a star athlete. Their paths crossed mostly on the football field where she rooted for him every week, but that changed one night in October 2008 when, Hillaire says, Rakheem Bolton raped her.

The accusation dropped like a bomb in Silsbee, Texas. Rumors flew that Hillaire made up the story, ashamed of a consensual act because Rakheem was black. The footballer insisted the sex was consensual and was cleared of rape—only to plead guilty to simple assault. His lawyer suggested that Hillaire (whose name *Newsweek* and The Daily Beast has published with her parents' permission) had been "asking for it." Hillaire was kicked off the cheer squad for refusing to cheer for Rakheem on the field. A petition was started in her favor, and former NFL cheerleaders spoke out.

The small town became a cauldron of racial and sexual hysteria.

Three years on, the case remains unresolved, the wounds not yet cauterized, the bitterness still palpable. Yes, most of the protagonists have moved on: Rakheem to a local college, according to his lawyer; the school principal out of the district; Hillaire, now 19 and living at home, no longer speaking to the press. (She spoke only through her parents for this article.) Her mother, Christena Soignet, continues to work—albeit somewhat awkwardly, as a teacher in the school district that her family has now sued.

Craig Soignet has not moved on. Hillaire's father has filed a seemingly endless raft of lawsuits, some of which have been dismissed as "frivolous" actions. He's even appealed the matter to the U.S. Supreme Court. He seeks justice, vindication, peace of mind. But there will be no harmony in Silsbee—population 6,600—anytime soon.

It all began on a cool weekend night in October 2008, when, police documents state, 16-year-old Hillaire got drunk at a house party with some classmates—buzzed on Bud Light and vodka shots. According to police reports, Hillaire had kissed a different boy that night, and had been captured on a cellphone camera kissing another girl. Sometime in the early morning hours, records state, she ended up in a dark room with four boys: Bolton, a 17-year-old running back, his wide-receiver teammate, and two minors. The minors told police they fondled Hillaire while she kissed Bolton. They claim she helped them take off her clothes.

Things soon went sour. "They pulled my shirt up and pushed my bra aside," Hillaire told police. ". . . Hands on my thighs were pushing my legs apart. I felt someone penetrating vaginally." From outside the door, a friend heard Hillaire yell "stop!" and "no!" With the help of two others, he kicked in the locked door, finding Hillaire curled up under a pool table crying, naked from the waist down. Police documents state there was a condom wrapper on the floor, and a broken window: three of the four boys had fled, one leaving behind his pants and cellphone. "They raped me," Hillaire cried, as the owner of the house—the mother of a student—called 911. Hillaire had never had sex before.

There's a sign-of the-times irony to the whole thing: In the Deep South, the word of a black athlete being taken over that of a white cheerleader. And yet, the legacy of racism runs deep in Silsbee. It is said that the entrance to Hardin County once boasted a street sign that read, "Niggers, don't let the sun set on your head." The once-sleepy logging town is about 30 percent black today, but remains profoundly segregated. "If Rakheem Bolton was born a white boy, this case would never have materialized—I'll go to my death on that," says the athlete's lawyer, Stella Morrison. "Come on, this is deep Southeast Texas. Racism runs deep here."

As multiple civil suits wend their way through the courts— including one that was partially overturned this week—the case remains volatile. A retired police sergeant who is a longtime sex-crimes lecturer in the local high school tells *Newsweek*/The Daily Beast that he was fired by the district because he made a passing reference to it in a presentation. "It only shows how much they need it," the sergeant says. (The Silsbee school superintendent, as well as his lawyer, declined to comment on that or

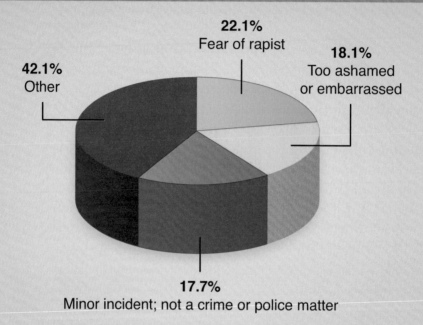

Percent of women who gave reason for not reporting a rape

22.1%
Fear of rapist

18.1%
Too ashamed
or embarrassed

42.1%
Other

17.7%
Minor incident; not a crime or police matter

Taken from: Sarah Morris. "Graph: Reasons for Not Reporting a Rape." *Columbia Missourian*, March 20, 2010.

any other matter related to this case.) As David Sheffield, the district attorney who prosecuted the first round of the case, puts it: "It's become a three-ring circus."

The fascination with this tale may have less to do with a single accusation and more with what it seems to represent: a window into the often twisted way we view rape victims in America and—in cases that often boil down to "he said, she said"—just how difficult such allegations are to prove. "It's a hard standard to begin with," says Ron Sullivan, the chair of the criminal law institute at Harvard Law School. "But we have a long history in this country of refusing to take sexual assault cases seriously—particularly in the so-called date rape context."

It's a scenario we've seen play out a thousand times. Girl accuses boy of rape. Girl is publicly discredited. If the boy is an athlete, there are all-too-often special efforts made to brush the problem under the rug. There are of course cases where the girl is lying. But more often, she doesn't even come forward: 60 percent of rapes go unreported. "It's typical," says Caroline Heldman, a professor of political science at Occidental College in Los Angeles, who has been writing on the Silsbee case for more than a year. "This is the only crime where the victim is consistently treated like a perpetrator. She is mocked, discredited, harassed, and this case is no different."

Indeed, the rumors flew in Silsbee: Had Hillaire made the story up? She didn't *look* like a girl who'd been raped.

But the most humiliating moment for the teen came not on the night of the alleged assault, or even on her first day back to school, where shrieks of "slut!" ricocheted in the halls. It came four months later, as she stood on the sidelines of a tournament basketball game, clutching a pompon in each hand.

Rakheem Bolton, charged with sexual assault after the attack but no-billed by a grand jury, headed to the free-throw line—he was a two-sport athlete. The cheer squad began its usual chant: "*Two, four, six-eight-ten!*" they yelled, bouncing in maroon and white. "*Come on, Rakheem, put it in!*" Hillaire winced, and stepped quietly out of the cheer line. She couldn't bring herself to cheer for the person she regarded as her attacker. "As a team, I cheered for them as a whole," she said later. But "when he stepped up to the line, it didn't feel right." At half time, her coach berated her, and a shouting match erupted. She was told she had to cheer "for everyone," or go home. She chose the latter. The following Monday, she was kicked off the squad. An irate Craig Soignet appealed to the superintendent; 11 days later, she was reinstated. But a war had begun.

Downtown Silsbee, or what's left of it since the Super Walmart moved in, sits in the center of Hardin County, less than 30 miles from Louisiana, but very much Texas. Dollar stores and check-cashing stands dot the highway, outnumbered only by churches. The community is deeply religious—and deeply loyal to the sports they call a "second religion." Bolton, say some locals, had helped put Silsbee on the map.

Craig Soignet has been a football season-ticket holder for more than 25 years. But he hasn't been to a game since Hillaire graduated from Silsbee High. Bolton pleaded guilty to a misdemeanor charge of assault nearly two years after the alleged rape, and was given a suspended one-year jail sentence, pending completion of an anger management course and community service. But it has not assuaged Soignet's outrage. He won't let it go.

Soignet keeps a detailed journal documenting every development. He's got a file cabinet full of recorded conversations with school officials and lawyers. He's got brochures for a half-launched support group for fathers of women who've been sexually assaulted; a stack of file folders full of education programs he hopes to persuade the school district to incorporate into its curriculum.

What kills him is that after all this time, he still feels nobody believes him. "In some ways, we'd all like to just move on from this," Soignet tells Newsweek/The Daily Beast from the office of his landscape and gardening business. "But if, God forbid, this happens to somebody else . . ." He trails off. "I just don't want any other person to have to go through what my daughter has."

The boys, though, dispute that Hillaire went through anything. They say it was she who pursued Bolton; that he and his friends fled out the window because they were scared—"the only blacks," as Bolton's lawyer puts it, "in a house of all whites." When Bolton returned that night to retrieve his clothes, police documents say, he shouted that, "I didn't rape no white girl!"

Hillaire spent the early morning hours of that night at a clinic with her mother, having a rape kit administered. The nurse who treated Hillaire, Brenda Garrison, says she found trauma to the vaginal area and bruising to the girl's hymen—all consistent, according to Silsbee Chief of Police David Allen, with sexual assault. Hillaire's mother says a bruise in the shape of a handprint would later form on the girl's upper thigh.

Even so, when Hillaire returned to school the following Tuesday—determined to keep her life as normal as possible—it was amid whispers that she "didn't look like a girl who'd been

In Silsbee, Texas, a cheerleader was kicked off the squad because she would not cheer for a player who she claimed raped her at a party.

raped." "He could have any girl he wanted," one commenter wrote of Bolton on a local blog. "He didn't need to rape no white girl." Craig Soignet says the school told Hillaire to "keep a low profile," and she spent more time at home than usual. She went to see a rape counselor weekly.

Under Texas law, a minor can't legally consent to sex—nor can a person who is intoxicated. But for a jury to believe that, says David Barlow, the special prosecutor on the case, a woman "practically has to be unconscious." According to police reports, Hillaire was sober enough to recount to officers what she said had happened, and Rakheem was within two years of her age. He would later tell the local press the whole thing was a big "misunderstanding." He has not spoken publicly since then, and did not respond to requests for comment.

Craig Soignet and his attorney, Larry Watts, have sued—unsuccessfully—everyone they can: the school district, the cheer sponsor, the superintendent and school principal, alleging they violated Hillaire's right to free speech by forcing her to cheer; the district attorney who first prosecuted the case, alleging he publicly discredited Hillaire when he told reporters that he "wasn't surprised" when the grand jury did not indict; as well as Bolton and his teammate, Chris Rountree, who allegedly helped hold Hillaire down. Most recently, the Soignets filed a federal Title IX complaint with the U.S. Office of Civil Rights, claiming Silsbee school officials had created a hostile educational environment when they allowed the person Hillaire had accused of raping her to remain in school. It was deemed beyond the statute of limitations, but they are appealing.

Soignet says it feels like his daughter was "raped, then raped again by the system."

The only break, of sorts, for Hillaire's family came this week, when a U.S. appeals court overturned part of a ruling that had ordered them to reimburse the school district for legal fees. Soignet and his lawyer are pressing on with appeals.

In the meantime, the youths accused in the case will continue to see their names bandied about on the Internet as "rapists." Hillaire's younger sister, a junior, left Silsbee High School last year for another facility, because she too was being harassed on campus. The Soignets say once-friendly neighbors now avoid eye contact.

They've thought about moving; making a fresh start. But they also refuse to give up in this town where they have deep roots: Christena's father was a city manager; her grandfather was a district judge. So they fight on—determined to remind people of a story everybody wants to forget.

"It's sad, because it feels like there are people all over the world who can sympathize with us, but not in our own community," says Craig, who wears a purple band around his wrist, in support of victims of sexual assault. "But if we can help one other girl, or one other father, it will all be worth it."

The question is whether—in a town that regards sports as a religious experience—his quest will ever be seen as more than a minor-league nuisance.

FOUR

Parties Are Likely Scenes for Acquaintance Rape

Marina Khidekel

> Marina Khidekel's article offers readers—both male and female—practical advice and warnings about party safety in high school and college. She points out that so-called party predators are not easy to spot but that any party involving alcohol consumption is a potentially dangerous situation. As Khidekel points out, the lines between sex and sexual assault are often blurred for both men and women; often both victims and perpetrators would never label their experience as rape. Awareness, advocacy, and caution—including looking out for one's friends—are the simplest strategies for safe partying.
>
> Marina Khidekel is an articles editor at *Glamour* magazine, overseeing the magazine's coverage of health and fitness. She has also contributed articles to *Seventeen*, *Teen Vogue*, *Allure*, and *Brides* magazines. Khidekel is the author of *The Quiz Life*, a book for girls that compiles popular quizzes from fashion magazines.

The party you're at is crowded, sweaty, and a lot of fun! The lights are dim, the music is loud, people are dancing, some people are drinking, there's a game of beer pong going on in the basement, and everywhere you look, guys and girls are flirting like crazy. You meet a cute guy—he's a friend of a friend, and he's really into you, complimenting you and showering you with attention. He's being a total gentleman, always making sure your cup is full. Then he suggests you two do shots. Before you know it, you're drunk. You didn't mean to get wasted, but suddenly you feel your body shutting down. But then when you wake up, he's on top of you, and your clothes are off. Wait, how did you get here? Did you agree to have sex with him? You don't think so, but it's hard to tell because you were just so out of it. You try to push him off, but you're too drunk to put up much of a fight. You just came here to dance and have a good time. This wasn't supposed to happen. . . .

Party predators are not easy to spot, and any party involving alcohol consumption is a potentially dangerous situation for females.

A party predator may be hard to spot—he could be a dude from calc class or a boy in your dorm who seems nice, normal, even sweet. But he's hiding a secret. Before a party gets going, he has planned out how he'll compliment you and flirt with you to

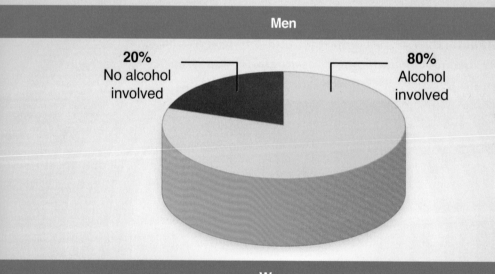

Alcohol as a Factor in Sexual Assaults at a Big Ten University

Men

20%
No alcohol involved

80%
Alcohol involved

Women

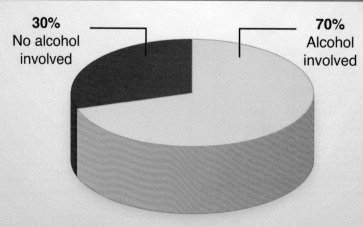

30%
No alcohol involved

70%
Alcohol involved

Taken from: IPFW, "Drug and Alcohol Information. www.ipfw.edu/police/drugs.

make you comfortable. Then he'll get you drunk so he can have sex with you—whether you want to or not.

"Girls have to understand that there are guys out there in high school and college who are ready and willing to take advantage of them," says Adam, 17, from Denver. Colorado. "I knew one guy who usually went after freshmen. He would invite them to parties, persuade them to drink, and then tell them that the coolest girls aren't virgins. Eventually, he would get them drunk enough to sleep with him, and I'm not sure that they all wanted to."

A Sketchy Situation

When a guy is throwing lots of attention at you, it makes you think that maybe it's the beginning of a real relationship. So you're into it, not realizing that it could be part of his plan. "When guys get all touchy-feely at parties, it's hard to get up the nerve to stop them," says Hannah, 18, from Stayton, Oregon. "In all honesty, if you are friends with them or you want them to like you, you don't want to risk getting them mad. Some guys will totally freak out if they don't get what they want: It's scary that guys you know could hurt you, and there won't be much you could do to prevent it."

A lot of girls feel like Hannah does, that it's a girl's fault for leading him on or making him mad, but the thing is—even if you were making out with him, even if you were drinking underage, even if you invited him up to your room, or you were wearing a sexy outfit, or you went to a party you weren't supposed to be at, if a guy has sex with you without your consent, it's rape.

You might think that the guys you know wouldn't do something so awful or that rape is only committed by violent strangers, but more than a third of people who have been raped were friends with the person who did it, according to the U.S. Department of Justice.

That's what happened to Camille, now 23, from Columbia, Missouri. "When I was 15, I went to a party at a friend's house," she says. "Her older brother got me drunk, and then all I remember is waking up in some bedroom without my underwear. People said I had sex with him, as if I'd wanted it to happen. But how could that be right, since I don't remember any of it? He took advantage of me."

Hazy Territory

It's not just girls who find all of this confusing. There are guys out there who can't clearly see the lines between sex and sexual assault—they admit that they think it's okay to have sex with a girl even when she's too drunk to say yes.

"Any woman who heads to a . . . party as an anonymous onlooker, drinks five cups of jungle juice, and walks back to a boy's room with him is indicating that she wants sex, okay?" wrote Alex, 20, an American University undergrad, in an editorial for his college paper last spring. And even when his essay sparked a massive backlash at his school, he wouldn't back down. "If you want to avoid risky situations, stay at home and watch *Twilight*," he added in a message to *Seventeen*.

Raising Awareness

That attitude seems pretty cold and frightening, doesn't it? But the good thing that came from Alex's editorial is that it got people talking. And the more people talk about it, the more they'll be aware of the problem so they can prevent it from happening again. Girls who have been targeted by party predators say that sticking by your friends and watching out for them is one of the best ways for everyone to stay safe.

Of course, not every guy is out to get you, but you need to know about potential dangers to be able to avoid them. Camille learned that the hard way. "We assume that people we know won't hurt us," she says. "We think that the men we associate with care about us—that they're invested in our well-being, just like our dads, our brothers, our boyfriends, or our childhood friends are. It's just not always the case."

FIVE

Wardrobe Choices Are Not an Invitation to Date Rape

Shira Tarrant

Outraged by a Toronto police officer's advice to students in early 2011 that "women should avoid dressing like sluts in order not to be victimized," groups of activists around the world started a series of so-called SlutWalks, demonstrations that aim to highlight the prevalence of sexual assault and debunk the idea that women who dress provocatively, including on dates and at parties, are "asking for it." These marches also provide public information about rape and sexual assault and help bring rape out of the shadows and into the public eye to raise awareness of the problem and the myths surrounding it. Shira Tarrant profiles the movement and the controversies and challenges surrounding it in the following viewpoint from a *Ms. Magazine* blog post.

Shira Tarrant received her doctorate in political science from the University of California, Los Angeles. She is an associate professor in the Women's, Gender and Sexuality Studies Department at California State University, Long Beach and the author of three books on gender issues.

"It's a dress, not a yes," is a rallying cry at the SlutWalk marches, which demand an end to rape and victim blaming. The movement started in January 2011, when a Toronto constable warned students that to avoid getting raped they shouldn't dress like sluts. Within months, anti-rape activists began taking to the streets in SlutWalks from New York to New Delhi.

"It's a dress not a yes" is more than a catchy rhyme. It means that what a woman (or a child or a man) is wearing is never an invitation to rape. Sexual assault is never caused by sartorial display. Too bad Charlotte Allen doesn't know that.

Allen is a contributing editor to the conservative Manhattan Institute think tank. On October 30, 2011, Ms. Allen wrote an OpEd for the *Los Angeles Times* equating women's skimpy SlutWalk outfits with sexy Halloween costumes, writing,

> *Feminists are in denial of a reality that . . . men's sexual responses are highly susceptible to visual stimuli, and women, who are also sexual beings, like to generate those stimuli by displaying as much of their attractive selves as social mores or their own personal moral codes permit.*

In response to Allen's politically negligent OpEd, writers such as Amanda Marcotte, Lindsay Beyerstein, Jill Filipovic, and Hugo Schwyzer lit up the feminist blogosphere with commentary and myth-debunking information.

More than Shock Value

SlutWalks are a spectacle to grab attention. The name alone makes people sit up and pay attention. But these marches do so much more than shock. SlutWalks provide information about sexual assault prevention and resources for recovery. SlutWalks are safe space to publicly speak out against sexual assault. People show up in sweatpants, jeans or everyday shorts, carrying signs that read, "This is What I Was Wearing When I Was Raped." They wear flip-flops, thigh-highs, clogs, and running kicks. A particularly heartbreaking sign held high at one SlutWalk announced, "I was raped when I was 4. I didn't know that footsies were slutty."

BECAUSE WE'VE HAD
ENOUGH

WALK, ROLL, HOLLER OR STOMP WITH US

SLUTWALK
CHICAGO

SATURDAY JUNE 4, 2011
12PM–3PM

**MAKE IT KNOWN THAT THOSE WHO EXPERIENCE
SEXUAL ASSAULT ARE NEVER THE ONES AT FAULT**

SLUTWALKCHICAGO.ORG
FACEBOOK: SLUTWALKCHICAGO TWITTER: @SLUTWALKCHICAGO

"Slutwalk Chicago Flyer," 2011. Reproduced by permission of Anthony Levin-Decanini.

The problem is that rape is compounded by myth—like when Charlotte Allen blames scantily clad women for provoking their own sexual assault. This ignores the fact that boys and men are also raped, and it is insulting to adult men everywhere. Men are not helpless slaves to their own sexual sight lines. Men have the power to make ethical, rational decisions about everyday matters, large and small.

Around the world women are forming demonstrations called "Slut Walks" to say that whatever they are wearing, it is not an invitation to sex.

Dangerous Misinformation

The problem is never what she (or he) is wearing—data shows that women are raped wearing running clothes, jeans, miniskirts, burqas and sweatpants. The real problem is dangerous misinformation about sexual assault that diverts our attention from finding good solutions.

The statistics about rape and sexual assault in this country should serve as a wakeup call. The United States has among the highest rate of rape among industrialized countries. Nearly two people are sexually assaulted every minute. About 17.6 percent of American women and three percent of American men experience attempted or completed rape at some point in their lifetimes. According to The National Center on Domestic and Sexual Violence, one in four girls will be sexually assaulted by the time they turn eighteen. For young boys, that figure is one in six. Yet only 26 percent of sexual assaults are ever reported to the police. Though most men do not rape, as anti-violence expert Jackson Katz points out in his book, *The Macho Paradox*, over 95 percent of rapes are committed by men, regardless of the victim's gender.

Yet as a society, we don't send a clear message about rape. A survey conducted by M. Koss, C. Gidycz and N. Wisnieweski found that one out of twelve college men had committed acts that met the legal definition of rape. Yet most of those men did not believe that what they did was rape. Toss together an alcohol-soaked culture with fuzzy understandings about sexual consent, and rape myths only add to this serious confusion about what constitutes a criminal act.

Changing Definitions

After eighty years of missing the mark, the FBI announced in January 2012 that it was finally revising its archaic definition of rape. Until then, the FBI only counted rape that included penetration of a penis into a vagina by force. That meant that coerced rape, men's rape, drugged rape, anal or oral rape, and rape by objects or fingers didn't even count as rape to the FBI. This revised FBI definition of rape includes any penetration, no matter how slight, of the vagina or anus with any body part or object, or penetration of the mouth by a sex organ of another person, without the consent of the victim. Now that our legal definitions of rape are improving, it is time to change our culture to one that would never dream of asking, "What was the victim wearing?" It is time we hold rapists and assaulters accountable because the question is never what was she wearing but why is he raping? This will remain the focus of SlutWalk when it returns to Toronto and to cities around the globe next spring. Perhaps, by then, pundits like Charlotte Allen will get a clue and fight rape instead of women.

It's time we are clear about what constitutes rape and it's time we respond appropriately. We need to change our culture to one that asks not, "What was the victim wearing?" but, "Why is he raping?" This will remain the focus of SlutWalk when it returns to cities around the globe next spring. Perhaps it can get the message across to pundits like Charlotte Allen: Fight rape, not other women.

SIX

Women Should Be Careful About How They Dress

Charlotte Allen

In the following viewpoint, Charlotte Allen identifies what she views as contradictions in the feminist position, including the recent SlutWalk anti-rape movement. She also takes on the idea that rape is about power and dominance rather than desire by pointing out that the majority of rape victims are young women. She compares a woman wearing provocative clothing to a man walking through a dark alley with a bulging wallet, and she advises younger women to avoid dressing like "faux-hos" in order to avoid inciting rape.

Charlotte Allen is a media fellow at the Manhattan Institute for Policy Research, a conservative think tank, and a contributing editor for the Manhattan Institute's Minding the Campus website on higher education. Her articles have appeared in many newspapers and magazines, including the *Atlantic*, *National Review*, *New Republic*, *Wall Street Journal*, and *Los Angeles Times*. She is also the author of the book *The Human Christ: The Search for the Historical Jesus*.

What do "SlutWalks," the anti-rape demonstrations that have been held in nearly every major city, and Halloween parties have in common? A lot. Both feature phalanxes of females flaunting scanty clothing that typically involves lingerie.

As everyone knows, the perennial favorite among Halloween costumes for women is "ho," followed by "sexy witch," "sexy nurse" and "Lady Gaga." So it's hard to spot the difference between the young woman marching down the street clad only in a lace corset and high heels for a SlutWalk and the young woman clad only in a lace corset and high heels for an evening of Oct 31 club-hopping. The only real difference is signage: The demonstrators often have the word "Slut" penciled on their foreheads or carry signs saying something like "My Clothes Are Not My Consent."

Here's an irony, though: The same feminists who promote SlutWalks as a protest against our supposed "rape culture," in which society always "blames the victim" for sexual assaults, are urging their sisters to cover up for Halloween. Take, for example, the feminist blog Feministing. Here is Feministing's founder, Jessica Valenti, writing in the *Washington Post* on June 3, not long after the very first SlutWalk, in Toronto: "[Y]es, some women dress in short, tight, 'suggestive' clothing—maybe because it's hot outside, maybe because it's the style du jour or maybe just because they think they look sexy. And there's nothing wrong with that."

But here is Feministing contributor Jessica Fuller, in an Oct 19 post titled "Eight Alternatives to 'Sexy' Halloween Costumes": "This Halloween try dressing for yourself, not the crowds." The eight "feminist" costumes listed by Fuller include Rosie the Riveter, Supreme Court Justice Sonia Sotomayor and Annie Hall. (A photo depicts a model attired like Annie in a fedora hat and a man's baggy pants, long-sleeved shirt, vest and tie: about as sexy as a bag of CornNuts.) If you must don a corset for that Halloween shindig, Fuller suggests you go as Gloria Steinem during her undercover stint as a Playboy bunny and "plan on using the inspired quotes you're sure to collect to write your own revolutionary essay."

Confusing Contradictions

The contradictory modes of the two women stem from a fundamental contradiction in the very idea of a SlutWalk. Back in the old days there were—as there still are—"Take Back the Night" rallies against the very same male-controlled culture that supposedly condones the sexual abuse of women. Since old-time feminists were in charge of Take Back the Night, the dress code was old-time feminist: bluejeans and T-shirts. Then this past spring a police constable in Toronto teaching a personal-safety class at York University said that "women should avoid dressing like sluts in order not to be victimized."

The admonition, if crudely put, was practical, rather like advising someone walking through a dangerous neighborhood at night not to flash expensive jewelry or leave a wallet hanging out. Sure, it's not your fault if you get mugged while flaunting your wealth, but you could have taken steps to reduce the risk.

A group of women in the class didn't see the remark that way, though, which led to the galvanizing of a young cohort of feminists, who accused the officer of "slut-shaming." Hordes of them painted "Slut" somewhere on their persons and took to the streets

"I GUESS YOU CAN'T SAY SHE'S ASKING FOR IT, BUT SHE DOES SEEM TO BE HINTING."

"I Guess You Can't Say She's Asking for It, but She Does Seem to Be Hinting," cartoon by Carroll Zahn. www.Cartoonstock.com

wearing little more than their push-up bras (and sometimes not even that). They waved signs reading "Don't tell us how to dress. Tell men not to rape." They wanted to make a point, as Valenti wrote, that "the sad fact is, a miniskirt is no more likely to provoke a rapist than a potato sack is to deter one."

The SlutWalkers got all huffy when people—including some old-time feminists—pointed out that their attire might be sending mixed signals, especially to men. A New York City SlutWalker who decided to protest rape culture by performing a pole dance on the sidewalk was quickly surrounded by male gawkers filming her on their phones.

People march at a Take Back the Night rally in Portland, Maine. The nationwide rallies seek to end violence against women.

Denying Realities

As illustrated by Valenti's remark, the SlutWalk feminists are in denial of a reality that is perfectly obvious to both the women who favor "sexy" for Halloween parties and (although perhaps not consciously) the SlutWalkers themselves. The reality is that men's sexual responses are highly susceptible to visual stimuli, and women, who are also sexual beings, like to generate those stimuli by displaying as much of their attractive selves as social mores or their own personal moral codes permit. In Victorian times that meant flashing an ankle every now and then. Now, it means . . . whatever. It's no wonder that SlutWalks have quickly outstripped (as it were) Take Back the Night as anti-rape protest. Women get another chance besides Halloween to dress up like prostitutes!

The other reality that feminists tend to deny is that rape and sexual desire are linked. Rape, in that view, is a purely political act of male dominance. This ignores the fact that the vast majority of rape victims are under age 30—that is, when women are at their peak of desirability.

Rape is a criminal act, and it is a crime most men won't commit regardless of how short a girl's skirt is or how lovely her legs. But the fact that rapists tend to target young women rather than grandmotherly types suggests that in the real rape culture (in contrast to the imaginary rape culture of some feminist ideology), the faux-hos of Halloween and their SlutWalker counterparts marching in their underwear—like a man walking at night with a bulging wallet—should be careful about where they flash their treasure.

SEVEN

Tests for Date Rape Drugs Have Advantages and Disadvantages

Jarrah Hodge

So-called date rape drugs such as rohypnol and GHB are tasteless sedatives that perpetrators use to spike intended victims' drinks at bars and parties. Recently, in many parts of the world, kits that allow women to detect the presence of common date rape drugs have become available. In the following viewpoint the effectiveness of these kits—which have names like the Drink Detective, Drink Guard, and Drink Safe Technology, is examined. This viewpoint, however, also brings up larger concerns about whether such tools might contribute to a culture of blaming the victim, if women fail to utilize such kits and fall victim to date rape drugs. Products like the Drink Detective raise questions about responsibility and liability for women's safety in dating and party situations, the author contends.

Jarrah Hodge is a blogger and writer based in Vancouver, Canada, whose interests include politics and women's studies. Her writing on gender and culture frequently appears in the *Vancouver Observer* newspaper, as well as in *Bitch Magazine*.

In July 2010, Canadian pharmacies started stocking the Drink Detective, a portable kit the size of a credit card that women can use to detect the presence of date rape drugs in their drinks. My first thought was that it's a great thing. When you go out, you lock your doors to prevent someone stealing your belongings. I didn't see how buying a date rape drug test kit was any different. At least two of my close friends have been date raped and I know that it not happening to me is due to dumb luck, not any real difference in behaviour. But maybe now there would be something I could do other than just watching my drink.

Two young women test their drinks for date rape drugs at a local tavern. Law enforcement fears that testing could lead to more assaults by creating a false sense of security.

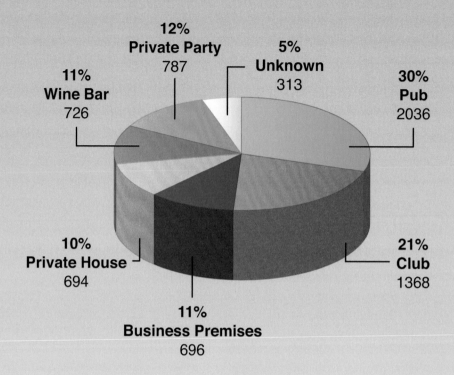

Places Date Rape Drugs Are Found

12%
Private Party
787

5%
Unknown
313

11%
Wine Bar
726

30%
Pub
2036

10%
Private House
694

21%
Club
1368

11%
Business Premises
696

Taken from: Drink Guard Drink Spike Detector. "Statistics." www.drinkspikedetector.com/statistics.htm.

But some organizations that work with women who have been raped think the kit might cause more of a problem than it solves. Although she agreed the test could be good if it helped protect women, Daisy Kler of Vancouver Rape Relief and Women's Shelter told PostMedia: "This is a cynical attempt to make some money, and shame on the company for feeding off the fear that women, reasonably, have of being raped. . . . By focusing on women's behaviour it gives the message that women can somehow prevent these attacks from happening and if they don't it's somehow their fault."

Another Reason to Blame Women

Kler is absolutely right that our society is at fault for sometimes blaming women for being raped. A few weeks ago a friend of mine was complaining about changes made to camping regulations at Merritt Mountain Fest. When I asked her why they'd made the changes, she replied, "Because a bunch of chicks were too stupid to watch their drinks and got themselves raped." I suggested maybe a different way of looking at it was that some stupid guys shouldn't have brought drugs and raped people. Her reply was, "Well, yeah. But girls should watch their drinks too."

That's what Kler and other victims' advocates are talking about. They're rightfully worried that if women don't use the Drink Detective, it'll give police and the public another reason to blame women for "getting themselves raped" instead of putting the blame on the rapists where it belongs. For their trouble, Vancouver Rape Relief and other groups that raised concerns about the Drink Detective were pegged as "hand-wringing" women's organizations by Ian Mulgrew in the *Vancouver Sun*.

A Useful Tool?

Mulgrew persuasively used examples of date rape cases that resulted in acquittals or dismissals of charges to argue that the Drink Detective "will do what the legal system has been unable to do—protect women from predators who spike their drinks."

While I didn't agree with Mulgrew's characterization of the organizations' opinions, his argument makes sense: better to protect yourself if you can than hope you might get justice after the fact. The problem is, in addition to potentially perpetuating a victim-blaming culture, the whole test may just not be as effective as its makers would like you to think.

Quebec pharmacist Maciek Zarzycki told CTV that the test may give false positives and noted that each test can only be used once. "So it's not really intended to test every single drink you're going to take in **a** bar. It's more for if you're suspicious about a drink." I'm not convinced I'd know the right time to feel suspicious about a drink, so I didn't find that reassuring.

More disturbingly, *Maclean's* magazine dug up a peer reviewed study on Drink Detective from 2006, which found that for every 100 drugged drinks, the test gave an average of 31 false negatives. For 100 clean drinks, the test averaged 12 false positives. Conveniently, the results of that study are left off the "Science" page of the Drink Detective website.

EIGHT

Date Rape Drugs Are Not as Common as Many Believe

Stephen Adams

> Many women believe that date rape drugs are common-place at bars and parties; so much so, Stephen Adams reports in the following viewpoint, that they rank them as more of a factor in sexual assault than drinking, knowingly taking drugs, or walking alone at night. Adams suggests, however, on the basis of a recent study published in a British scientific journal, that alcohol—ingested know-ingly by the victim—was actually far more of a factor than rohypnol or GHB, which showed up only very rarely in the blood samples of sexual assault victims. Perhaps, sug-gests Adams, date rape victims who claim to have been under the influence of so-called date rape drugs were actu-ally just intoxicated by alcohol.
>
> Stephen Adams is the medical correspondent for Britain's *Telegraph* newspaper. In addition to covering medical news, he has written about arts and culture.

A study of more than 200 students revealed many wrongly blamed the effects of a "bad night out" on date-rape drugs, when they had just drunk excessively. Many are in "active denial" that drinking large amounts of alcohol can leave them "incoherent and incapacitated", the Kent University researchers concluded. Young women's fears about date-rape drugs are so ingrained that students mistakenly think it is a more important factor in sexual assault than being drunk, taking drugs or walking alone at night.

The study, published in the *British Journal of Criminology*, found three-quarters of students identified drink spiking as an important risk—more than alcohol or drugs. More than half said they knew someone whose drink had been spiked. But despite popular

Despite the popular belief that date rape drugs are prevalent, law enforcement says they have found no evidence that date rape victims are usually drugged.

beliefs, police have found no evidence that rape victims are commonly drugged with such substances, the researchers said.

Not the Real Threat

Dr Adam Burgess from the university's School of Social Policy, Sociology and Social Research, said: "Young women appear to be displacing their anxieties about the consequences of consuming what is in the bottle on to rumours of what could be put there by someone else.

"The reason why fear of drink-spiking has become widespread seems to be a mix of it being more convenient to guard against than the effects of alcohol itself and the fact that such stories are exotic—like a more adult version of 'stranger danger'." Rituals to protect drinks from contamination, such as taking drinks to the lavatory in clubs and bars and buying only bottled drinks, have become commonplace, the academics noted. Among young people, drink spiking stories have attractive features that could "help explain" their disproportionate loss of control after drinking alcohol, the study found.

Maintaining Control

Dr Burgess said: "Our findings suggest guarding against drink spiking has also become a way for women to negotiate how to watch out for each other in an environment where they might well lose control from alcohol consumption." Co-researcher Dr Sarah Moore said: "We would be very interested in finding out whether the urban myth of spiking is also the result of parents feeling unable to discuss with their adult daughters how to manage drinking and sex and representing their anxieties about this through discussion of drink spiking risks."

Nick Ross, chair of the Jill Dando Institute of Crime Science, commented: "There is no evidence of widespread use of hypnotics in sexual assault, let alone Rohypnol, despite many attempts to prove the contrary." During thousands of blood and alcohol tests lots of judgement-impairing compounds were discovered, but they were mostly street drugs or prescription pharmaceuticals taken by

"Pint of lager and a rohypnol shandy please mate."

"Pint of Lager and a Rohypnol Shandy Please Mate," by Clive Goddard. www.Cartoonstock.com

the victims themselves, and above all alcohol was the common theme. As Dr Burgess observes, it is not scientific evidence which keeps the drug rape myth alive but the fact that it serves so many useful functions." Dr Burgess and his team questioned more than 200 students at universities in London and south east England. . . . [In 2011], Australian researchers found that not one of 97 young men and women admitted to hospital over 19 months to two Perth hospitals claiming to have had their drinks spiked, had in fact been drugged.

NINE

Feminists Define Rape Too Broadly

Alex Knepper

In this viewpoint, prompted by a previous opinion piece in the *Eagle*, the American University student newspaper, *Eagle* columnist Alex Knepper articulates an extremely controversial standpoint regarding date rape: that a college woman who drinks excessively and then goes to a male classmate's dorm room has little right to accuse him of date rape after sex. He suggests that sex is a volatile arena and that the lines between rape and consensual relations have grown increasingly blurred due to labels such as date rape, which, Knepper argues, is not adequately defined. Knepper argues for a more multifaceted discussion and definition of sex and consent.

Alex Knepper graduated from American University in 2011. He has written for the *Frum Forum*, *NewsRealBlog*, and other blogs, and his provocative writing on topics (such as rape and child molestation) has frequently stirred discussion and debate. The article presented here, which was originally published in the campus newspaper of American University, sparked student protests and ultimately led to Knepper's resignation from the paper.

Jeremiah Headen likely lost the vice presidency of the Student Government over a hyperbolic Facebook note.

Its contents—a blast of old-school masculinity—slammed men for not realizing that being manly had nothing to do with what is between one's legs, but rather is about values, stoic resolve and hard work. It ended with a silly, all-caps call to raid booty and women from neighboring villages.

The comments on *The Eagle's* Web site, mostly by Gay Party activists and feminists, condemned Headen for being an "anti-queer misogynist" and for undermining American University's commitment to being "safe space" for the "gay community." He was also rebuked for using the term "hermaphrodite" instead of "intersex."

What a sniveling bunch of emotional cripples! I have never encountered a more insular, solipsistic view of human sexuality than at this college. The rigidity of Pat Robertson has nothing on feminism. Feminist religious dogma, long ago disposed of by neuroscientists and psychologists, states that men are essentially born as eunuchs, only to have wicked masculinity imposed on them by an evil society. This is usually presented as "social construction theory."

Spoiling Sex

Like the other great religions of the world, though, the goal of contemporary feminism and Gay Party activism is not to explain sex, but to abolish its passion. The yin and yang of masculinity and femininity is what makes sexual exploration exciting. Sex isn't about contract-signing. It's about spontaneity, raw energy and control (or its counterpart, surrender). Feminism envisions a bedroom scene in which two amorphous, gender-neutral blobs ask each other "Is this OK with you?" before daring to move their lips any lower on the other's body. Worse yet: a gender-neutral sexual-

Reported Forcible Sex Offenses at Ten Largest US Campuses, 2008–2010

School	Enrollment	Forcible Sex Offenses, 2008–2010
University of Minnesota	52557	36
Arizona State University	59794	12
University of Central Florida	58587	8
Ohio State University	56867	42
University of Texas at Austin	51112	23
University of Florida	49589	8
Texas A&M University	49861	10
Michigan State University	47800	38
Pennyslvania State University	44485	23
University of Michigan	42716	45

Numbers represent offenses on campus and in residence halls.

Compiled by Editor.

ity can have no conception of the inherently gendered thrills of fetishism, sadomasochism, kink or cross-dressing. How blasé! For my pro-sex views, I am variously called a misogynist, a rape apologist and—my personal favorite—a "pro-date rape protofascist."

"An Incoherent Concept"

Let's get this straight: any woman who heads to an EI [Epsilon Iota fraternity] party as an anonymous onlooker, drinks five cups of the jungle juice, and walks back to a boy's room with him is indicating that she wants sex, OK? To cry "date rape" after you sober up the next morning and regret the incident is the equivalent of putting

The author asserts that women who get drunk, go to bed with a man, and then wake up the next day saying they have been raped have no reason to complain.

a gun to someone's head and then later claiming that you didn't ever actually intend to pull the trigger.

"Date rape" is an incoherent concept. There's rape and there's not-rape, and we need a line of demarcation. It's not clear enough to merely speak of consent, because the lines of consent in sex—

especially anonymous sex—can become very blurry. If that bothers you, then stick with Pat Robertson and his brigade of anti-sex cavemen! Don't jump into the sexual arena if you can't handle the volatility of its practice!

Feminists don't understand history, psychology, biology or sexuality. To repair this desperate situation, I have altruistically prepared a list of five favored books about sex and gender: *The Myth of Male Power* by Warren Farrell, *The Sexual Spectrum* by Olive Skene Johnson, *Vamps and Tramps* by Camille Paglia, *Philosophy In the Bedroom* by the divine Marquis de Sade, and *Who Stole Feminism?* by Christina Hoff Sommers. Put down the Andrea Dworkin and embrace the fires of sexuality!

TEN

Some Women Can Find Date Rape Difficult to Recognize

Patti Feuereisen

Although date rape can happen to anyone at any time, therapist Patti Feuereisen suggests that young women who have a history of sexual and emotional abuse often are more vulnerable to putting themselves in situations where date or acquaintance rape is likely to occur or to ignoring the warning signs of date rape. Here she shares a graphic story from Iris, one of her clients, who was raped after a night of clubbing during college. Iris's story illustrates not only the circumstances that can contribute to date rape (heavy drinking, lack of friends' supervision) and her inability or unwillingness to label her experience as rape but also the benefits for rape survivors of entering therapy to understand their experiences.

Patti Feuereisen is a clinical psychologist who practices in New York City. She specializes in working with girls and young women who are victims of sexual abuse, and she has started a scholarship program, GirlThrive, for sexual abuse and incest survivors. Feuereisen is the author of *Invisible Girls: The Truth About Sexual Abuse*.

I met Iris when she was twenty-two and a senior in college. She had been raped three years earlier but had only recently come to terms with the fact that it was even a rape. In fact it was a male friend who convinced her that what she had experienced was date rape.

Since the rape, she had been in a string of bad relationships with men who did not appreciate her. She came to therapy because she had a sense that her rape of three years earlier had affected how she made choices in relationships. She also wanted to deal with her history of emotional abuse and connect the dots as to why she kept picking such losers.

Abused as a Child

Iris had not been physically sexually abused as a child, but she had been emotionally and verbally sexually abused and also physically abused by her older brother. Iris comes from a Jewish family. She is the younger of two children; her brother is seven years her senior.

Both of their parents worked and her brother was left in charge of her beginning when she was seven and he was fourteen. That was when he started abusing her verbally. He would repeatedly taunt her. He would choke her, pinch her, make sexual comments about her breasts, her hips, and her rear end, and constantly tell her that she was a "worthless, ugly piece of shit." By constantly talking to her in sexual terms and touching her in inappropriate ways, her brother taught her that she had no right to any boundaries, physical or emotional.

What She Deserved

As a child, Iris didn't know how to stop the sexual innuendoes or the inappropriate touching. Of course, in front of their parents, her brother behaved like an angel. Her parents trusted and praised their son, and when Iris complained about how he mistreated her, they ignored her.

When Iris began dating at around fifteen, she seemed to seek out males who would treat her badly. In hindsight, of course, that's no surprise. That's what she knew; that's what she felt she deserved. She put herself into many situations she should never have been in and struggled through adolescence with the feeling that she didn't deserve good relationships.

Fast forward. Iris is now twenty-two and graduating at the top of her class from a prestigious university. She came in to see me because of her recurring nightmares, heightened anxiety, and depressive feelings. She had hit bottom and wanted to understand why she kept having dreams about the rape.

In Iris's story, she tells what it's like to be out partying with your friends and what can happen as you get more and more drunk or high, how your judgment can blur, and how quickly your situation can escalate and get dangerous.

She talks about how she would get "buzzed" to deal with her insecurities and her very human need to fit in, and then describes the date rape and its aftermath. . . .

Iris's Story

I was nineteen years old and had just finished my first year of college. A group of us were going out to celebrate the end of exams and the beginning of summer. We met at a club I had never been to. I loved the magic that took place when you entered a club. Through those guarded portals lay another world, a planet with an atmosphere all its own. Our group of three young women and two young men entered a room with swarms of people dancing to music, and I squinted as my eyes adjusted to the darkness. My head was fuzzy from the drinking I'd already done that night.

Our group met up with some other friends I did not know. There were people everywhere, drinking, talking, popping pills. I was immediately attracted to a guy named Michael. He smiled a sweet, boyish smile when introduced to me and I noted how handsome he was. He had large, dark eyes and a narrow goatee. I smiled back at him, more from self-consciousness than anything else. When I'd left the house that night I'd thought I looked good, but when I looked at the people around me, they seemed to have stepped out of the pages of a fashion magazine. I felt like an impos-

Symptoms of Post-traumatic Stress Disorder

1. Recurrent, persistent, and distressing reexperiencing of the trauma
2. Persistent avoidance of stimuli that remind of the trauma
3. Amnesia
4. Numbing of general responsiveness
5. Increased irritability, hypervigilance, trouble concentrating
6. Social and occupational impairment

Taken from: DSM-IV.

tor in the velvet-drenched, smoky scene. For more courage, I got another drink at the bar.

The bartender was a friend of a friend and had made us something special on the house. Sweet, fruity drinks usually made me sick, but I took a large gulp. It went down surprisingly smoothly, and I swallowed the rest of it quickly before my buzz had a chance to disappear. I wanted to drown myself in the stuff, let the pink liquid rise above my head as I danced and the alcohol pounded in my brain as if keeping time, my limbs gaining courage with every sip. Michael came over and danced with me. He was holding my back and swaying slowly from side to side, and my body responded. He was strong and my lightness felt secure in his arms. The music got faster and I started to move on my own in a sensual, drunken haze. He smiled down at me, grinding back. I was absorbed in the moment, in a capsule, all by myself. No external reality existed for me. All I knew at that moment was how good I felt, how good and free and light.

A Scary Turn

We stopped dancing and got another drink and started talking, and I found him as charming and funny as he was handsome.

My friends then joined us. Ezra, a guy I had some classes with, came over and put his arm around me. He had been Michael's friend since high school, and after a while Ezra and Michael said, "Wanna get out of here?" I said good night to my girlfriend, who was also pretty drunk, and she winked at me, and we left.

My head was spinning wildly now, and I was starting to lose my balance. I should have listened to what my body was telling me, to have them drop me off at home so I could sleep the drunkenness off. I was drunk and tired, but I trusted Ezra and I was attracted to Michael. I was dizzier than ever, slightly nauseous and stumbling, but I still thought I was all right. Michael and Ezra took me by the arms and held me up, and we stood there, in front of the club, waiting for a taxi to take us home.

The next thing I knew, I was in bed in my apartment with no idea how I'd gotten there. My head felt like a swarming beehive and as I opened my eyes, I saw Ezra crouched over me. He kissed me, the dry, alcoholic taste of his mouth mingling with mine, but I was dizzy. I wasn't aroused. I couldn't feel anything. Then, as quickly as he had begun, Ezra stopped kissing me. He pulled his face away from mine and looked down at me again. Michael came over. . . .

I was so confused. . . . I couldn't respond. Then Ezra appeared above me. I could feel my legs being pried apart and Michael sticking his face between them as Ezra shoved his tongue in my mouth. My body was numb and I felt nothing, as if my nerve endings had been severed. As the drunken fog in my head began to clear, I realized what was happening. With the little strength I had, I got up and away from them and ran into the bathroom.

"Like a Rag Doll"

I was crying hysterically when Ezra came in. "What's the matter, baby?" he asked. I couldn't stop crying, couldn't talk, my body was shaking as I tried to speak. I tried to explain to him that I didn't know what was happening, that I was drunk and didn't want to do this. "Don't cry, baby, don't cry. I thought you liked Michael. You really want us to stop?" I nodded my head yes, suddenly exhausted, and he said okay, leaving me alone in the bathroom. The next thing I knew I was lying on the bathroom floor alone, with closed eyes, having passed out again. My body was leaden, too heavy to move, and I wasn't sure where I was. The alcohol seemed thicker in my bloodstream now, moving slow as syrup, disorienting me. Before I could figure out where I was next, I felt my underwear being pulled off my body.

Realizing this was no dream, I opened my eyes and found Ezra gone. I had been dragged out of the bathroom and pulled to the floor in the bedroom and Michael was kneeling in front of me. He was pulling my legs up around him.

. . . I was so tired I was paralyzed. I felt like a rag doll, a limp creature with no skeletal structure or will of my own. It felt as if he was splitting me in half. I was torn between numbness and pain, and I asked him to stop. I opened my mouth to say no, but he rammed his tongue into my mouth hard. He kept pounding into me. I faded in and out, unable to stay awake. I kept trying to push him off me, I kept crying and struggling, and at one point I managed to get away.

I ran into the kitchen and hid behind the refrigerator. I was huddled back there shaking like a frightened animal. He followed me in and pulled me from behind it, lifting me like a feather. . . . Finally he carried me back to bed to finish what he'd started. I realized I wasn't going to get away and I almost willed my body to stay limp so I could disappear.

Aftermath

When he was done, he rolled over. I was allowed to fall back to sleep. I passed out from fear, exhaustion, and shock. When I woke up, the sun was up and I heard noises in the apartment. I found myself on the floor. Michael was at the edge of the bed. He seemed large and awkward, mean-spirited, uninterested. He was putting on his shoes.

"Hey, do you have a T-shirt I can borrow?" he asked.

I looked at him for a minute, confused, before lifting myself up from the floor. I rummaged through my dresser drawers for

Iris shared her story because she believes that girls should look out for one another and not get drunk or stoned to the point where they make themselves vulnerable to danger.

something that would fit him. "Thanks," he said, barely glancing up. Suddenly I felt ashamed. He continued dressing. I felt stupid and pathetic, and frightened at the same time. He wasn't friendly; he wasn't nice at all. He grabbed his knapsack from the messy floor, littered with clothes—my clothes from the night before.

"See ya," he said, slamming the door behind him.

I stood for a moment watching the door, amazed that he could have disappeared so quickly. Tears were suddenly falling from my burning eyes. I smelled like smoke and my mouth was dry and pasty, my vagina was bruised and burning, and bleeding. There was dried blood all over my legs. The remnants of the alcohol were nauseating me. My inner thighs ached, and my lower back stung. I saw bruises on my upper chest and my legs. I crawled back into bed, trying to figure out what had happened. All I wanted was for someone to tell me it would all be all right. I wanted to be held tenderly. I pulled the covers high over my head and lay like that for a long time, until I finally cried myself to sleep.

Facing the Truth

It took me a long time afterward to recognize what had happened to me. Unable to face the truth, I said to myself that I had been "rejected," a much easier pill to swallow than having been date-raped. I didn't talk about the experience to anyone. I basically put the incident in the back of my mind. I would run into Ezra from time to time, but he acted as if nothing had happened.

About one year after the incident I was describing it to a friend and he said, "Iris, you were raped!" I can honestly say that it hadn't hit me until then. I had been date-raped.

Three years after the incident, at twenty-two, I began therapy. I didn't know where to start. So I started to rehash the abuse I had experienced at the hands of my older brother. I began to understand that I had believed his lies; I had believed that no one would want me, so I was susceptible to any attention. In retrospect I think I kept drinking that night because I was insecure and wanted Michael to like me. I came to therapy because I knew I needed to change. I was feeling insecure about graduating and finding a job, I was having nightmares, and my therapist explained that I needed to appreciate myself before I could commit to any relationship.

In the past two years, my therapy has been a journey to some places I didn't want to go. But I am finding that the more I talk about my childhood abuse at the hands of my brother and the lack of support from my parents, the more I am able to begin to stop blaming myself. As children we have little to no control over the violations of our families—verbal, sexual, or physical—yet as young women we can choose friends and lovers that do not treat us as our families did.

I have since learned that I do have boundaries. I have since learned that it is my responsibility, and no one else's, to make sure people respect me. As a child I could not control my destiny. I could not get my parents to see the demoralization I had suffered at the hands of my brother. But as an adult I get to choose to be around good people. I don't have to speak with my brother. I can limit my time with my parents if they are unsupportive. Slowly but surely, I am putting the rape behind me. I am learning that I am worth more. I have begun to heal.

My Thoughts

Iris very much wanted to share her story to help other young women avoid the mistake she made. She wants girls to know that they should not get drunk or stoned to the point where they make themselves vulnerable to danger. We also learn from her story that sometimes young women don't watch out for each other.

As she tells us, Iris did not have high self-esteem, and even though she was not physically molested as a child, the torment she suffered from the emotional and physical abuse by her brother brought her to a point where she believed she deserved very little in relationships. It is no wonder Iris responded to the attention of these two males. After all those years of being told how ugly she was, just a crumb of positive attention felt great.

You'll recall that she knew, as she was getting drunk, that she didn't have all her faculties, but she trusted her "friend" Ezra. In fact she drank so much that she passed out and came in and out of consciousness during the rape. She was so ashamed, she didn't even want to blame the rape on Ezra and Michael; it was easier to tell herself she'd been rejected by Michael.

I've seen many other girls who've blamed themselves for date rapes. They figure they're old enough that they should be able to keep things from getting out of hand. That's why date rape on college campuses is such a huge problem. Within the past ten years, date rape on college campuses has been identified as the number one problem, with date and acquaintance rape topping the list of violent crimes against women on college campuses. And although in the past ten years we have made some progress by bringing this crime to the forefront, it remains a huge problem.

Many college girls are testing their new freedom; they do want to go out and get drunk and have a good time; they may even really be into the guy who takes them home. But that doesn't mean they asked to be raped. If a girl resists or says no or tries to run and a guy overpowers her, that is rape. All the backlash writing in the world doesn't change that fact.

Ask yourself a few questions: Is Iris's story so different from what could have happened to you on a night of partying? Do you and your friends keep each other's backs? Do you keep an eye on your drink at all times to be sure no one tampers with it? If there is ever a time where you can prevent being violated, date rape is it.

ELEVEN

Acquaintance Rape Is Still a Big Problem on College Campuses

Tina deVaron

In the following viewpoint, a woman who attended Princeton University in the 1970s—shortly after the university became coeducational—reflects on her own experience of date rape in college and on whether the university has made advances in addressing this problem in the decades since then. Her story illustrates that even though awareness and openness about rape have improved over the past thirty years, the atmosphere of male sexual dominance and violence toward women still underlies many facets of campus life. She argues that men, women, and institutional leaders need to take a stronger stand against even so-called innocent fun that contributes to a rape culture on campus.

Tina deVaron is a singer, songwriter, and jazz pianist. She performs arrangements of jazz for children during her "Tunes with Tina" shows, and she has also released several albums of original songs about motherhood.

The recent "She Roars" conference at Princeton celebrated 42 years of coeducation and featured such powerhouse alumnae as Justice Sonia Sotomayor, former eBay CEO Meg Whitman, and Teach for America founder Wendy Kopp. When

I entered Princeton in 1973, the university had been coed for four years. Now, it was hosting a celebration of women's empowerment, unveiling a landmark study on undergraduate women's leadership.

On the conference's opening night, a female a cappella group, the Princeton Tigerlilies, gave a concert. The girls sang prettily, dressed in short black frocks and high pumps. Then the group's all male a cappella counterpart, the Nassoons, performed. For the song "ShamaLama," they serenaded one of the Tigerlilies onstage, with choreography: In rhythm, they pantomimed unzipping their flies, and bluntly thrust their pelvises forward at the lone young woman on stage. Sixteen guys, one girl. The guys smirked, the girl smiled meekly.

I am an ex-director of a collegiate a cappella group. As are my husband and both of our sons. We're steeped in the traditions and humor. But this was worse than tacky. Women around me were agape with disbelief. Should we have been surprised, with Yale being sued for its frat boys chanting "No means yes," and headlines on alleged sexually predatory behavior dominating the news? Despite decades of women's "empowerment," male sexual prerogative is alive and well in our society, and among these Princeton undergrads.

Remembering a Rainy Night in 1973

My She Roars schedule showed no events addressing this kind of hostile environment or date rape—and only a glancing reference to sexual assault in the "Undergraduate Women and Leadership" report. I began feeling angry. Because of the way my own life had changed at Princeton during freshman year. On a rainy night, whose events I'd suppressed for years until hearing a report about date rape on NPR [National Public Radio] brought it back.

Following a big exam, my resident advisor (RA) treated his rugby friends and me to a beer at a neighborhood roadhouse. After we returned to the dorm and said our goodnights, there was a knock at my door. The rugby team captain asked if he could

Young women today find that college attitudes still define an atmosphere of male sexual dominance and violence against women.

sleep on my roommate's vacant bed, since it would be such a rainy walk up campus.

I still don't know why I let him in. I was not drunk; I remember every minute of the next hour. I said no, he said yes. I struggled; he was the rugby player. When he had finished raping me, he went back to his dorm in the rain. I remember him calling the next day to "see how I was." I remember hearing people laughing in the background. He was the friend of my RA, someone I respected. It didn't make sense. I told no one. I stayed in my nightgown the whole next day. For years I thought that by letting the guy in, I was somehow complicit in the crime.

A Culture Largely Unchanged

I wonder about the climate for Princeton women now, where girls smile prettily while sixteen men pantomime what is essentially gang rape, in front of an audience of middle-aged women, many of them moms. Sexual conquest for a nineteen-year-old man is one step on the ladder to success. Not so for the nineteen-year-old girl who did not consent.

When the memories of my incident surfaced, I called my pastor. She had had a similar experience as an undergrad. How many others are keeping this hidden?

I am lucky, married to a man who respects and loves me, and the mother of two sons who are self-aware gentlemen. Why not simply be grateful for this wonderful conference at my alma mater, filled with brilliant women and old friends? Why write about this now? Because I still carry the events of 37 years ago with me, as will many women who have been raped. And because there is a girl reading this now who will be starting at Cornell in the fall, or Penn State, or Miami, who will be entering an environment largely unchanged from the Princeton campus I walked onto nearly four decades ago.

It's a culture where "no still means yes." It's a culture where male sexual dominance (and violence) underlies daily interactions, frat parties, and even a cappella concerts. Skeptics might protest, "They were only having harmless fun. Those guys aren't rapists." But it's precisely this kind of attitude of sexual conquest that entitles men to rape women. And there's nothing harmless about that.

How Campuses Entitle Men to Rape

The date rape statistics speak for themselves. One in four women will be sexually assaulted on a college campus. Between 15 and 30 percent of college women have been victims of acquaintance rape at some point in their lives. And these aren't violations at the hands of strangers on the street. According to the National Victims Center, 84 percent of women know their assailant. And 57 percent of rapes occur on a date. For women victims ages 18

Reported Forcible Sex Offenses at Ivy League Schools, 2008–2010

School	Enrollment	Forcible Sex Offenses, 2008–2010
Brown University	8649	23
Columbia University	22920	23
Cornell University	20633	7
Dartmouth College	6141	44
Harvard University	20699	63
Princeton University	7592	42
University of Pennsylvania	20643	25
Yale University	11666	30

Numbers include offenses on campus and in residence halls.

Compiled by Editor.

to 29, two-thirds know their attacker. And more than 60 percent of rapes occur in residences.

That's the reality we're sending our bright college women into. In context, the antics of those college a cappella boys aren't the stuff of innocent comedy. Those moves are representative of a larger culture that accepts and desensitizes us to sexual violence against women. I keep asking myself: Why was there nothing in Princeton's She Roars conference that addressed this? College campuses can no longer afford to be complicit in this culture. Women—*and* men—need to take a stand to change the language, the behaviors, the relationships, the clubs, and the institutions that allow it.

The benefit will be a wiser, more open, more equal society in general. And perhaps the men's a cappella performance at the next She Roars conference will not be quite so tone-deaf.

What You Should Know About Date Rape

Key Statistics About Date Rape:
- According to One in Four, Inc., one in four college women have been the victims of rape or attempted rape.
- According to the National Center for Victims of Crime, 85 percent of college women who were raped knew their assailants.
- The National Center for Victims of Crime states a woman is four times more likely to be raped by an acquaintance than by a stranger.
- A national study of college students found that one in twelve male students surveyed had committed acts that met the legal definition of rape.

Common Myths About Date Rape:
- Rape is only committed by strangers.
- Women who wear provocative, sexy clothing deserve to get raped.
- Women who do not physically fight back have not really been raped.
- If no weapon is involved, then it is not really rape.
- If it is a boyfriend or husband, or they have had sex before, it is not rape.
- If a woman lets a man buy her dinner, she "owes" him sex.
- Only women are raped.

Common Date Rape Drugs
Rohypnol
- Rohypnol is the trade name for flunitrazepam.
- It is similar to two other drugs, known by the brand names Xanax and Klonopin.
- Rohypnol comes as a pill that dissolves in liquids. It may also be ground into a powder before being added to a drink.
- Newer pills include a dye that turns bright blue in liquids; however, this color change might still be hard to see in a dark drink or in a dark room.
- Rohypnol may be known by many nicknames, including "Roofies," "R-2," or "Poor Man's Quaalude."

GHB
- GHB is short for gamma hydroxybutyric acid.
- It may be produced as a pill, a liquid, or a white powder.
- It has a slightly salty taste that may be masked by a sweet drink.
- GHB is also known by nicknames such as "Liquid X," "Vita-G," or "Cherry Meth."

Ketamine
- Ketamine is either a liquid or a powder.
- It is particularly fast acting and also causes memory problems.
- It may be known as "Kit Kat" or "Special K," among other nicknames.

Alcohol
- Alcohol is actually the substance most commonly used to help commit sexual assault. It is important to remember that even if a victim drank alcohol or willingly took drugs, it is *never* the victim's fault for being assaulted.

How Young Men Can Prevent Date Rape
According to the nonprofit advocacy group Men Can Stop Rape, boys and men can do several key things to prevent rape.

- Ask before you act.
- Accept when consent is not given or is withdrawn.
- If a person is too high or drunk to give consent, wait until you are both sober before moving forward.
- Designate a friend to keep an eye out for signs of sexual violence at parties and to intervene if required.
- Let friends know that jokes about rape and sexual violence are never funny.

What You Should Do About Date Rape

It is important for everyone to remember that being assaulted is *never* the victim's fault. That being said, there are things you can do to help reduce your risk of rape when on a date.

Reduce Your Risk

The first thing is to communicate clearly and consistently. Express your limits clearly and repeat them if necessary. In addition to speaking clearly, speak and act in an assertive manner. Do not be afraid to share your feelings confidently and even forcefully if the situation calls for it. Be as alert as possible. Remember that alcohol and other drugs can impair your judgment and your all-important ability to communicate. And be prepared. Always carry extra money and your cell phone with you so that you are not dependent on your date for a ride. Meet your date in a public place such as a coffee shop, movie theater, or restaurant until you know and trust him well.

Avoid Date Rape Drugs at Parties

There are also things you can do to help reduce your risk of date or acquaintance rape at parties. Even if you know you are going to be consuming alcohol, there are things you can do to help protect yourself. First, do not drink anything that you did not open yourself or see poured. Once you have your drink, always keep an eye on it; date rape drugs can easily be added to unattended drinks and are often difficult to detect. Although some date rape drugs are tasteless and odorless, be alert for bitter tastes in a mixed drink, which may indicate the presence of date rape drugs.

Do not go to parties alone. Make a deal with your friends to watch out for each other, intervening if you see your friends making poor decisions. If you suspect a friend has been drugged because she's acting far more inebriated than her level of alcohol consumption would suggest, do not leave her alone. And if you suspect you have been drugged, immediately ask your friends or someone you trust for help and get to a public place if at all possible.

Raise Awareness

Talk to your school's nurse or guidance counselor about planning an event or series of events to raise awareness about date rape. Post statistics about date rape around your school, along with 800 numbers for rape hotlines. Consider inviting rape victims and crisis counselors to speak at a school assembly, and follow it with an assembly about healthy sexuality and gender roles. Hold a series of self-defense workshops. Organizations such as Take Back the Night and RAINN offer many suggestions for hosting events during April (Sexual Assault Awareness Month) and throughout the year.

Self-Defense

Although it's important for victims not to blame themselves, there are things young people can do to help protect themselves. These common-sense techniques include things like carrying a cell phone on a date or at a party or club, and making sure someone else knows where you are and who you are with.

If you would like to know how to protect yourself even more, consider signing up for a self-defense class for young women. Although sometimes the most effective defense is making noise or just running away, self-defense classes can help teach basic techniques for fighting back. Most importantly, though, these kinds of training programs can just help improve self-confidence for young women in potentially risky situations. High schools, colleges, gyms, and communities often hold these kinds of training programs.

Positive Peer Pressure

Both young men and young women can help change the culture of rape in high schools and colleges by not only condemning the behavior but also promoting more positive role models of masculinity and supporting an environment of respect toward women. A young man may feel under immense pressure to have sex on a date so that he can brag about it to his friends or just to feel accepted or admired by others; downplaying those kinds of "conquest" stories can help change a sexually aggressive atmosphere, one locker room at a time.

If You or a Friend Have Been Raped

According to the DC Rape Crisis Center and the Santa Monica Rape Treatment Center, there are important steps you should take as soon as possible if you have been the survivor of any kind of rape or sexual violence. First, go to a safe place and contact someone you trust. Report the crime to the police if you want to, and preserve all physical evidence of the assault. You may need to seek medical attention at a hospital or clinic; a medical examination is important if you think you might want to press charges. Also write down as much as you can remember about the assault; your account may be important evidence if you press charges, and even if you do not, doing so can help clarify your thoughts and feelings.

Talking about what happened is also really important. Call a friend or a rape crisis hotline. If you talk to a doctor, nurse, or the police, do not be afraid to ask questions or get information about what you can and should do next. Finally, recovering emotionally from an assault can take months or years. Consider talking with a crisis counselor or other mental health professional.

ORGANIZATIONS TO CONTACT

The editors have compiled the following list of organizations concerned with the issues debated in this book. The descriptions are derived from materials provided by the organizations. All have publications or information available for interested readers. The list was compiled on the date of publication of the present volume; names, addresses, phone and fax numbers, and e-mail and Internet addresses may change. Be aware that many organizations take several weeks or longer to respond to inquiries, so allow as much time as possible.

Arming Women Against Rape and Endangerment (AWARE)
PO Box 242
Bedford, MA 01730
(781) 893-0500
e-mail: info@aware.org
website: www.aware.org

AWARE's mission is to educate the public and individuals about personal safety issues. The organization offers a variety of training programs in self-defense, including courses for women in the use of handguns, aerosol sprays, and other personal defense tools. AWARE offers training for individuals as well as for law enforcement professionals, social workers, rape crisis centers, and other nonprofits. Its website offers quizzes about self-protection and stalking, as well as information on self-defense and common crimes.

Men Can Stop Rape
1003 K St. NW, Ste. 200
Washington, DC 20001
(202) 265-6530
fax: (202) 265-4362
e-mail: info@mencanstoprape.org
website: www.mencanstoprape.org

Men Can Stop Rape was founded in 1997; its mission is "to mobilize men to use their strength for creating cultures free from violence, especially men's violence against women." The group offers educational programming and clubs for preteens and teenagers, as well as college students, and it also produces awareness materials for the public at large. The organization's website offers numerous resources for both perpetrators and survivors of sexual assault as well as links to other men's antiviolence organizations. Many handouts on topics such as supporting survivors and rape as a men's issue are available for download on its website.

National Center on Domestic and Sexual Violence (NCDSV)
4612 Shoal Creek Blvd.
Austin, TX 78756
(512) 407-9020
e-mail: dtucker@ncdsv.org
website: www.ncdsv.org

Formed in 1998, the National Center on Domestic and Sexual Violence has the goal of ending domestic and sexual violence through training, consultation, and policy advocacy. The NCDSV offers professionally led training and consulting for law enforcement agencies, other businesses, and the military. The center's website includes numerous links to recent news items dealing with issues of sexual and domestic violence.

One in Four
10 Shirlawn Dr.
Short Hills, NJ 07078
e-mail: info@oneinfourusa.org
website: www.oneinfourusa.org

One in four college women have survived rape or attempted rape. That's the statistic behind the name of this nonprofit organization that focuses on educational programming for university and military settings. One in Four offers programs for both men and women, and according to its website, sexual assaults are proven to decrease on campuses on which students have taken these educational programs.

Pandora's Project
3109 W. Fiftieth St., Ste. 320
Minneapolis, MN 55410
e-mail: admin@pandys.org
website: www.pandorasproject.org

The mission of Pandora's Project is "to provide information, facilitate peer support and offer assistance to male and female survivors of sexual violence and their friends and family." It has an extensive online support community, including a message board and chat room, as well as other social networking options. In addition to these online sources of support, Pandora's Project's website offers numerous links to online resources as well as to other organizations working in this area.

Rape, Abuse, and Incest National Network (RAINN)
2000 L St. NW, Ste. 406
Washington, DC 20036
(800) 656-HOPE (-4673)
e-mail: info@rainn.org
website: www.rainn.org

RAINN is the nation's largest anti-sexual violence organization. RAINN operates a national sexual assault hotline, both on the phone and online, and it offers numerous education and advocacy programs. Its website includes common-sense information for young people, as well as information on student activism and social networking actions.

Sisters of Color Ending Sexual Assault (SCESA)
PO Box 625
Canton, CT 06019
(860) 693-2031
website: www.sisterslead.org

SCESA addresses sexual violence issues by examining the underlying issues of social injustice and silence that disproportionately affect women of color. It partners with other organizations for advocacy and education, and it offers training and consultation nationwide for organizations and communities interested in more fully exploring these issues.

Victim Rights Law Center (VRLC)
115 Broad St., 3rd Fl.
Boston, MA 02110
(617) 399-6720
fax: (617) 399-6722
website: www.victimrights.org

Founded in 2000 as a project of the Boston Area Rape Crisis Center to advocate legally for the rights of sexual assault victims, the Victim Rights Law Center now provides legal representation for survivors and advocates nationwide for victims' justice in criminal and civil cases. The VRLC trains attorneys nationwide to do this type of work; in 2009, VRLC staff trained more than two thousand professionals and victims' advocates across the country. The VRLC's website includes resources for vicims and legal advocates, as well as links to news stories and a free e-newsletter.

BIBLIOGRAPHY

Books

Joanna Bourke, *Rape: Sex, Violence, History*. Emeryville, CA: Shoemaker & Hoard, 2007.

Kerry Cohen, *Dirty Little Secrets: Breaking the Silence on Teenage Girls and Promiscuity*. Naperville, IL: Sourcebooks, 2011.

Todd Denny, *Unexpected Allies: Men Who Stop Rape*. Bloomington, IN: Trafford, 2007.

Jennifer L. Dunn, *Judging Victims: Why We Stigmatize Survivors, and How They Reclaim Respect*. Boulder, CO: Lynne Rienner, 2010.

Maria Ochoa and Barbara K. Ige, *Shout Out: Women of Color Respond to Violence*. Emeryville, CA: Seal Press, 2007.

Vanessa Place, *The Guilt Project: Rape, Morality, and Law*. New York: Other Press, 2010.

Liz Seccuro, *Crash into Me: A Survivor's Search for Justice*. New York: Bloomsbury, 2010.

John J. Sloan III and Bonnie S. Fisher, *The Dark Side of the Ivory Tower: Campus Crime as a Social Problem*. New York: Cambridge University Press, 2010.

Sarah E. Ullman, *Talking About Sexual Assault: Society's Response to Survivors*. Washington, DC: American Psychological Association, 2010.

Periodicals and Internet Sources

Charlotte Allen, "Death by Political Correctness: Who Killed Antioch College?," *Weekly Standard*, November 12, 2007.

Jane E. Brody, "The Twice-Victimized of Sexual Assault," *New York Times*, December 12, 2011.

Sewell Chan, "'Gray Rape': A New Form of Date Rape?," *New York Times*, October 15, 2007.

Susan Greene, "Rape Victim Deserves Answers," *Denver Post*, October 17, 2010.

Bob Karlovits, "How to Stay Safe on a College Campus," *Pittsburgh Tribune- Review*, August 31, 2009.

Victoria P. Lowe, "Saving a Stranger," *Cosmopolitan*, August 2008.

Alicia Montgomery, "Date Rape: Blame It on the Alcohol?," National Public Radio, April 15, 2010.

Tony Norman, "Date Rape Drug Cases Cry for Attention," *Pittsburgh Post-Gazette*, July 15, 2011.

Robert Nott, "Voice to a 'Muted Crime,'" *Santa Fe New Mexican*, August 23, 2011.

Al Renna, "Sexual Assault Can Be Prevented," *Winston-Salem (NC) Journal*, April 11, 2011.

Joseph Shapiro, "Campus Rape Victims: A Struggle for Justice," National Public Radio, February 24, 2010. www.npr.org.

Laura Sessions Stepp, "A New Kind of Date Rape," *Cosmopolitan*, September 2007.

Stockton (CA) Record, "Clearly Defined: You Can't Make Distinction Between Types of Rape," June 7, 2009.

Jennifer Torres, "Pacific Targets Date Rape," *Stockton (CA) Record*, March 29, 2011.

Kate White, "How to Stay Safe from Sexual Predators," *Cosmopolitan*, December 2008.

Malinda Williams, "Everybody's Business: College Campus Life and Date Rape," *Taos (NM) News*, August 27, 2009.

Women's Health Weekly, "MU Researcher Calls for Increase in Sexual Assault Awareness Programs on College Campuses," January 1, 2009.

Sana Yaseen, "She Was Raped. On Her Dream Date," *DNA*, March 21, 2010.